MW01010048

# WHAT A
*Friend* WE HAVE
IN JESUS

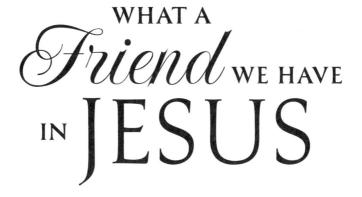

# WHAT A *Friend* WE HAVE IN JESUS

## CHIEKO N. OKAZAKI

DESERET
BOOK

SALT LAKE CITY, UTAH

© 2008 Chieko N. Okazaki

All rights reserved. No part of this book may be reproduced in any form or by any means without permission in writing from the publisher, Deseret Book Company, P. O. Box 30178, Salt Lake City, Utah 84130. This work is not an official publication of The Church of Jesus Christ of Latter-day Saints. The views expressed herein are the responsibility of the author and do not necessarily represent the position of the Church or of Deseret Book Company.

DESERET BOOK is a registered trademark of Deseret Book Company.

Visit us at DeseretBook.com

Library of Congress Cataloging-in-Publication Data

Okazaki, Chieko N., 1926–
  What a friend we have in Jesus / Chieko N. Okazaki.
    p. cm.
  ISBN: 978-1-59038-855-6 (hardbound : alk. paper)
  1. Christian life—Mormon authors. 2. Jesus Christ—Mormon interpretations.
3. Mormon women—Religious life. I. Title.
  BX8656.O49 2007
  248.4'89332—dc22                         2007043847

Printed in the United States of America
Publishers Printing, Salt Lake City, UT

10  9  8  7  6  5  4  3  2  1

*For Kenneth and Kelle*
*Robert and Chris*

# CONTENTS

# 1

## "What a Friend We Have in Jesus"

*P*erhaps you've heard the popular Protestant hymn "What a Friend We Have in Jesus." I learned it as a girl growing up in Hawaii, and it was a favorite hymn of my dear husband, Ed, who was raised as a Congregationalist. Even though it's not in our LDS hymnbook, you're probably more familiar with it than you might think. Here are the first few lines:

> What a Friend we have in Jesus,
> All our sins and griefs to bear!
> What a privilege to carry
> Everything to God in prayer!

The hymn tune by Charles C. Converse is the same as that of "Israel, Israel, God Is Calling," with words by Richard Smyth. Now, if you think about these two hymns together, they make a wonderful pair. "Israel, Israel, God Is Calling" is a grand old missionary hymn that invites those who are seeking the truth to come out of Babylon and the temptations in those "lands of woe" and find shelter with the Saints in Zion. As a convert myself, I know that sense of crossing a threshold from one world into another and finding a new home in Christ's church.

But once we're in Zion, are our troubles over? Hardly! That would confuse Zion with the celestial kingdom. In fact, as every one of you knows, it is in the intimate, trusting environment of our marriages, our families, our wards, and our neighborhoods—the places of the most intense longing and belonging—where we are also most vulnerable to injury and being wounded.

There is in an older edition of our LDS hymnal a warning to those who assume "all is well in Zion." It is a hymn we don't sing anymore, but perhaps we should. It is entitled "Think Not When You Gather to Zion," and it reads in part:

> Think not when you gather to Zion,
> That all will be holy and pure;
> That fraud and deception are banished,
> And confidence wholly secure. . . .
> No, no; for the great prince of darkness
> A tenfold exertion will make,
> When he sees you go to the fountain,
> Where freely the truth you may take.
> (*Hymns* [1948], no. 21)

If I may be personal for a moment, Ed and I moved to Utah in 1951 as a young married couple, just a couple of years out of college. I had been a member of the Church since I was fifteen, but Ed had joined the Church ten months after we were married. We were both of Japanese ancestry, and World War II had been over for only six years. That's not very much time to forget categories such as "enemy" or "Jap" or "foreigner." Many households in Utah were still suffering the grief of having lost a father, son, or brother in World War II, many of them in the Pacific Theater. Furthermore, there was a long history in the United States of legal discrimination in housing, jobs, and education against non-Caucasians.

So Ed and I understood why it was hard for people to look past our skin color and slanted eyes to our smiles and our hearts. We heard many hurtful things. We had to deal with the fact that we couldn't get car insurance or buy a home and that even at church, people hesitated to approach us. Ed and I said many times to each other, "If we were going to lose our testimonies, it would be right here in the heart of Zion." So even though we were part of the Israel that had been called out of Babylon and even though we had come to Zion, our troubles were far from over.

And that's perhaps why we loved this hymn, "What a Friend We Have in Jesus," and heard its echoes every time we sang "Israel, Israel, God Is Calling." Here are the rest of the words to that wonderful hymn:

> Oh, what peace we often forfeit,
> Oh, what needless pain we bear.
> All because we do not carry
> Everything to God in prayer!
>
> Have we trials and temptations?
> Is there trouble anywhere?
> We should never be discouraged;
> Take it to the Lord in prayer.
>
> Can we find a friend so faithful,
> Who will all our sorrows share?
> Jesus knows our every weakness;
> Take it to the Lord in prayer.
>
> Are we weary and heavy-laden,
> Cumbered with a load of care?
> Precious Savior, still our refuge!
> Take it to the Lord in prayer.
>
> Do thy friends despise, forsake thee?
> Take it to the Lord in prayer.
> In His arms He'll take and shield thee;
> Thou wilt find a solace there.

Let me share a little bit about the man who wrote this powerful expression of faith in Jesus Christ's infinite and unfailing love. His name was Joseph Scriven, and he was born in Ireland in about 1820. When he was twenty-five, his fiancée drowned the day before their wedding.

Reeling from the tragedy, he made up his mind to immigrate to America. Packing up his belongings in Dublin, Ireland, he sailed for Canada, leaving his mother behind. . . .

Ten years later, in 1855, he received word that his mother was facing a crisis. Joseph wrote this poem and sent it to her. Mrs. Scriven evidently gave a copy to a friend who had it published anonymously, and it quickly became a popular hymn, though no one knew who had written it.

Meanwhile, Joseph fell in love again, but tragedy struck a second time when his bride, Eliza Catherine Roche, contracted tuberculosis and died in 1860 before their wedding could take place.

To escape his sorrow, Joseph poured himself into ministry, doing charity work for the Plymouth Brethren and preaching among the Baptists. He lived a simple, obscure life in Port Hope, Canada, cutting firewood for widows, giving away his clothes and money to those in need. He was described as "a man of short stature, with iron-gray hair, close-cropped beard, and light blue eyes that sparkled when he talked." Ira Sankey later wrote:

Until a short time before his death, it was not known that he had a poetic gift. A neighbor, sitting up with him in his illness, happened upon a manuscript copy of "What a Friend We Have in Jesus." Reading it with great delight and questioning Mr. Scriven about it, he said that he had composed it for his mother, to comfort her in a time of special sorrow, not intending that anyone else should see it. Some time later, when another Port Hope neighbor asked him if it was true he composed the hymn, his reply was, "The Lord and I did it between us."

On October 10, 1876, Joseph became critically ill. In his delirium, he rose from his bed and staggered outdoors where he fell into a small creek and drowned at age 66. His grave was arranged so that his feet were opposite those of his lost love, Eliza Catherine Roche, that at the resurrection they might arise facing one another.[1]

It is plain to me that Joseph Scriven had not one but two tests of his faith that were possibly the cruelest that a man can face. In the case of his first fiancée's death, he might easily have murmured or wondered why the Lord did not intervene to spare her from drowning or alert someone who could have saved her. In the second case, again hoping for the happiness of married love, he again lost his fiancée. Why hadn't the Lord healed her? But instead of losing his faith, to the end of his life, he believed, as his actions showed, that he truly trusted in the Lord and strove to live a Christian life of service to others.

Is there anything that we cannot take to the Lord in prayer? Is there anything that we *should* not take to the Lord in prayer? I, with this humble and faithful soul, Joseph Scriven, testify that there is not. But I want to share with you some thoughts about why we sometimes hesitate to "take it to the Lord in prayer." I think there are three main obstacles. First, we feel that we should be able to solve our own problems. Second, we aren't specific in asking for exactly what we need. And, third, we need to be willing to see the answer coming as a process, line upon line, precept upon precept.

## Being Self-Sufficient

The gospel teaches us that we should be anxiously engaged in a good cause and bring to pass much righteousness of our own free will and bring to pass much righteousness (see D&C 58:27). Sometimes we interpret this to mean that we should solve our own problems and only go to the Lord as a last resort. I remember reading a story about a woman named Connie, who had extreme problems in her life.

> [A friend] asked Connie how she was able to bear up under the load of such troubles. Connie replied, "I take my problems to the Lord."
>
> Connie's friend replied, "Of course, that is what we *should* do."
>
> Then Connie added, "but we must not only *take* our problems there. We must *leave* our problems with the Lord."
>
> [Then she told a story about] . . . an elderly man who vowed he would never ride in an airplane. However, one day an emergency arose and it was necessary for him to get to a distant city in a hurry. The fastest way to get there was by air, of course, so he purchased a ticket and made his first flight in an airplane.
>
> Knowing his reluctance to fly, when his relatives met him at the airport, they asked him how he enjoyed the flight. He responded, "Oh, it was all right, I guess. But I'll tell you one thing. I never let my *full weight* down on the seat."[2]

Did this elderly gentleman's tense balancing on the edge of his seat make him weigh less in the airplane or make him any less dependent on the airplane's strength to hold him up? No, of course not. It only prevented him from trusting the plane and the pilot, relaxing, and enjoying this new experience in his life.

We so often hear the proverb, "The Lord helps those who help themselves," that we sometimes think it's in the Bible. It isn't. What *is* in the Bible is "Trust in the Lord with all thine heart; and lean not unto thine own understanding. In all thy ways acknowledge him, and he shall direct thy paths" (Proverbs 3:5–6).

Trusting in the Lord and taking *all* our burdens to him in prayer does not mean that we become passive or helplessly dependent. It means that we become peaceful. The Apostle Paul promised: "Be careful for nothing; but in every thing by prayer and supplication with thanksgiving let your requests be made known unto God. [Then] the peace of God, which passeth all understanding, shall keep your hearts and minds through Christ Jesus" (Philippians 4:6–7). When we trust, we are not in a state of inattention. We are attentive to the whisperings of the Spirit. That is how we can hear accurately and respond appropriate and quickly.

I've forgotten where I read this, but I was very struck by someone who noticed that the Lord also has a 9–1–1 number. It's the first few verses of Psalm 91:

> I will say of the Lord, He is my refuge and my fortress: my God; in him will I trust. . . .
>
> Under his wings shalt thou trust: his truth shall be thy shield and buckler.
>
> Thou shalt not be afraid for the terror by night; nor for the arrow that flieth by day;
>
> Nor for the pestilence that walketh in darkness; nor for the destruction that wasteth at noonday.
>
> A thousand shall fall at thy side, and ten thousand at thy right hand; but it shall not come nigh thee. . . .
>
> Because thou hast made the Lord, which is my refuge, even the most High, thy habitation; . . .
>
> For he shall give his angels charge over thee, to keep thee in all thy ways. (Psalm 91:2, 4–7, 9, 11.)

If we believe this, then we must also believe that God has not only the power to help us but also the will. I believe he most sincerely and earnestly desires our well-being. That he yearns to bless us. That he is reaching out toward us, offering the strength and the shelter of his loving arms. So maybe, just maybe, we can get over thinking that we need to do it all ourselves.

## Pray in Specifics

Second, I think a frequent obstacle is that we need to be more specific in our prayers, not just expressing an all-purpose plea such as "give us this day our daily bread" and hoping that God will know it really means, "money to replace the snow tires on the Toyota before the first blizzard." Alma counseled his people: "[Ask] for whatsoever things ye stand in need, both spiritual and temporal; always returning thanks unto God for whatsoever things ye do receive" (Alma 7:23). That sounds all-inclusive to me.

Sometimes—and this is funny if you think about it—we feel shy about telling the Lord what we really want and need because we feel that our concerns are too trivial to bother the Savior of the world with. At that point, I think we need to remember the lines from Joseph Scriven's hymn that say: "What a *privilege* to carry, / Everything to God in prayer!"

When Apostle Orson F. Whitney was a young man serving a mission in Great Britain, he was assigned to the mission home in Liverpool to edit the mission magazine. There he learned an important lesson about prayer:

> I found myself in an overworked, run-down condition, manifesting a decided lack of physical and mental vigor. . . . One morning I was endeavoring to write the usual editorial but could make no headway, and wore out the whole day in a vain attempt to produce something worth reading. At last I threw down my pen and burst into tears of vexation.
>
> Just then the Good Spirit whispered: "Why don't you pray?"
>
> As if a voice had addressed me audibly, I answered, "I do pray." I was praying five times a day—secret prayers, morning, noon and night; and vocal prayers, with the rest of the household, at breakfast and dinner time. "I do pray—why

can't I get some help," I asked, almost petulantly, for I was heartsick and half-discouraged.

"Pray now," said the Spirit, "and ask for what you want."

I saw the point. It was a special not a general prayer that was needed. I knelt and sobbed out a few simple words. I did not pray for the return of the Ten Tribes nor for the building of the New Jerusalem. I asked the Lord in the name of Jesus Christ to help me write that article. I then arose, seated myself, and began to write. My mind was now perfectly clear, and my pen fairly flew over the paper. All I needed came as fast as I could set it down—every thought, every word in place. In a short time the article was completed to my entire satisfaction.[3]

There are times of emergency when we have only time to pray, "Please help me!" But I think, with Brother Whitney, that when we are specific about exactly what we need, we allow our Heavenly Father to honor our agency and meet that specific need.

### Learn Line upon Line

The third obstacle I want to mention is the opposite of these first two. Sometimes we view prayer as a sort of magic. We expect to drop a prayer in and out pops an answer. I've had miraculous answers like that, but I've also wrestled for the answer to my prayer like Jacob wrestling with the angel—not because God could not have instantly answered my prayer but because I needed to go through the process of learning line upon line, precept upon precept.

Let me share an example from when I served in the Relief Society general presidency. In doing so, I am talking not only about a miracle for me, but also a miracle for you.

When I was called to the presidency, President Gordon B. Hinckley set me apart. He said, in that blessing:

We feel to say unto you that you bring a peculiar quality to this presidency. You will be recognized as one who represents those beyond the borders of the United States and Canada and, as it were, an outreach across the world to members of the Church in many, many lands. They will see in you a representation of their oneness with the Church.

We bless you that you may be free in speaking, that your tongue may be loosed as you speak to the people.

I bear witness that President Hinckley's blessing has been literally fulfilled. I do not speak Korean or Spanish or Tongan. But when I received my assignments to go among the Relief Society sisters and their priesthood leaders in those places, I was filled with a great desire to speak to them in their own language, and I felt Heavenly Father's approval of my desire to serve them in this way.

With the help of the Church translation department and good coaches who spent hours working with me, I was blessed to deliver my addresses in Spanish, Korean, and Tongan as I went among those people. I could feel the Spirit carrying my words to their hearts, and I could feel the Spirit bringing back to me their love and their faith, which strengthened me in my responsibilities.

Spanish and Tongan weren't too difficult, but Korean was a special challenge. In Korea, in sixteen days, our schedule required us to travel to eleven different cities, speaking to thirty-seven general meetings, workshops, leadership meetings, and smaller groups. I knew that there would not be a moment to waste, and I desperately wanted every moment to count. I also knew that Japan had long been a military and political adversary of the Korean people and that as a result of some of that history, there lingered bad feelings between Koreans and Japanese. As a woman of Japanese descent, I had a burning desire to express my concern and love for my Korean brothers and sisters. I wanted to speak to them directly from my heart without an interpreter. I wondered if I'd be able to read my address in Korean if I could learn the pronunciation given to the vowels and consonants. So I asked Brother Mackelprang of the Church Translation Department to translate the talk for me and give me some tutoring in how to form the consonants and vowels. He did more than that. He had his wife, who is Korean, tape the talk for me so that I could play it over and over, listening to how she pronounced the words.

I practiced and practiced and prayed and prayed. But something was wrong. The sounds weren't meaning anything to me and they weren't sticking in my head. Several times I thought, *Oh, just give it up. Let the interpreter do it.* But my desire to speak to the people directly was strong within me. I went through many steps in trying to read the language. One morning, I woke up early and was thinking about this problem again and praying for help. A voice came into my mind that said, *Write out the talk in Hiragana.*

You know that Japanese, Korean, and Chinese are completely different spoken languages but that both the Japanese and the Koreans borrowed Chinese characters to create their writing systems. It's something like the fact that we use the same alphabet to write words in English, French, Italian, Swedish, and German, although each language has some symbols that represent distinctive pronunciations. On the face of it, it wouldn't make sense to write out the Korean talk in Japanese Hiragana symbols because they'd be a string of nonsense syllables in Japanese, not coherent thoughts. Wouldn't it just distract me?

But the idea had come to me with such force that these logical thoughts didn't deter me. I immediately jumped out of bed, sat down at my desk, and using the Romaji—the English transliteration of the Korean talk—began writing them in Hiragana. It was absolutely amazing. At first, I had to labor, picking my way through and thinking hard about what I was doing, but it became easier and easier, paragraph by paragraph. By the end of the third page, I understood Korean. I understood its pronunciation. I understood its grammatical structure. I understood its intonation. Everything I had been practicing and practicing without feeling a sense of order or clarity about it suddenly made perfect sense. I couldn't *speak* Korean, but I could *read* Korean, and that was what I had prayed for.

When we reached Korea, the area president, Elder Eugene Hansen, warned us, "I know you have workshops planned. You need to know that the Korean people are very reserved and very quiet. They will be very attentive, but don't expect too much response and don't be disappointed if no one asks questions or volunteers answers in your sessions."

I was very concerned. As the program was arranged, I would speak first to the workshop through an interpreter. What if there were no response? Would I have the courage to try reading my talk in Korean at the general session without an interpreter? I prayed very hard.

During the workshop, I coached them to respond to me. For example, I would say, "One of the goals of Relief Society is to build personal testimony, right? Yes or no?" and they would nod. I would insist, "Yes or no?" They would say, "Yes," and laugh. And I would say, "Very good!" It was like being a cheerleader, assuring them that they were doing the right thing in answering. By the end of my introductory remarks, they were laughing and answering me.

Then during the part of the workshop that required brainstorming and small group participation, there was much laughter and very eager responses. Whenever I asked a question, there were hands raised all over the room. When I asked them to form small groups to discuss certain problems, they immediately complied. As I walked around the room, I saw priesthood leaders and Relief Society leaders talking earnestly together, listening to each other, sharing thoughts, sometimes so excitedly that they could barely wait for someone to finish before they added their own thoughts. Elder Hansen was astonished. He said, "I've never seen anything like this before, Chieko."

Then came the next test—the general session. I sat on the stand

and prayed while I was being introduced. Then I stood up alone, no interpreter. The people settled down to listen. I could see a few of them exchange puzzled glances, then smile as I began my introductory remarks. I knew that they thought I had memorized the greeting and that the interpreter would soon join me. But I kept going. Suddenly, everyone was sitting up, leaning forward. They were staring at me. Their mouths dropped open. They looked at each other disbelievingly. As I continued, tears came to their eyes. They listened with their whole hearts. That chapel was so quiet you could have heard a pin drop. I felt a spirit rise within me, a spirit of love, of energy, of connectedness. I could feel the words coming as though it was not I who was speaking them, and I could see, on the faces of the people before me, their comprehension of the words.

They came to me after the meeting, some of them weeping and unable to speak. Elderly women pressed my hands and groped for words. Many of them said, "Thank you," but the declaration that I prized most deeply was from the women who said, "You are like us!" That was the message of the heart that I wanted to convey. I *was* like them. They *were* like me. We were sisters in the gospel.

Elder Han In Sang, a Korean member of the Second Quorum of the Seventy, took me aside and asked, "How did you do it? How could you read Korean if you can't speak Korean?" I explained the process I'd gone through, and he was dumfounded. He couldn't figure out how that process would work, but he and I both knew that it was not the process. The members thanked me over and over. They said, "We have learned from you. We have learned that in doing and trying, blessings will come."

This miracle was performed on my behalf because my calling presented me with an opportunity I felt prompted in my heart to embrace and with a challenge I literally did not know how to surmount. Whether in your calling, in your family, in your profession, or in dealing with a personal problem such as addiction, a phobic reaction, or mental illness, you may also need a miracle in your life.

The point I want to convey from my experience is that, first, I took it to the Lord in prayer and he taught me, line upon line, precept upon precept, idea upon idea—even when rationally and logically I didn't see how the ideas that came to me one at a time could possibly work. Joseph Scriven's hymn affirms, "We should never be discouraged; / Take it to the Lord in prayer."

## Conclusion

Remember where we began? We began with "Israel, Israel, God Is Calling" and discovered that we can also sing "What a Friend We Have in Jesus" without missing a note. Then we explored three of the obstacles that sometimes keep us from taking *everything* to the Lord in prayer.

The first of those obstacles is our internal feeling that we must be self-sufficient, that even when we're in the airplane we should never let our weight down fully on the seat. Remember the Lord's 9–1–1 number. He has given his angels charge over us. We've got help we don't even know about.

The second of those obstacles is that we sometimes don't tell the Lord *exactly* what we are seeking. Remember Orson F. Whitney praying generically for "help" and wondering why he wasn't getting any, until the Spirit instructed him, gently and clearly, to pray for exactly the help he needed: clarity of thought and expression in writing the editorial that was, at that very minute, on his desk.

And the third obstacle is that we sometimes tend to fall back on magical, push-button thinking, wanting our blessings delivered to us in neat little packages that we just need to open. We need to realize that our prayers are sometimes answered in the "some assembly needed" and "batteries not included" mode. We need to be prepared to struggle as Jacob did, wrestling for our blessing.

Then think about me and my strong desire to speak to the Korean Saints in their own language and how I was led, one step at a time, line upon line, precept upon precept, to discover a method that, if you looked at it logically, made no sense at all.

Lastly, remember that Jesus is a *friend*. He doesn't care if we're praying with curlers in our hair, runs in our panty hose, and hysteria in our hearts. He just wants us to bring him everything in prayer: "all our sins and griefs," . . . our "needless pain," our "trials and temptations," our "every weakness," and our cumbering "loads of care." Like the much-tried but ever-faithful Joseph Scriven and our own prophets, I bear testimony that I have gone daily—and many times daily—to the Lord in prayer. In His arms he has taken and shielded me. I testify that I have found my solace there, and I promise that you will, too.

# 2

# "And Came Seeing"

he phrase "and came seeing," comes from one of the miraculous healings Jesus performed. When he anointed the eyes of a blind man with spittle and mud and sent him to wash in the pool of Siloam, the man faithfully and obediently did as he was told "and came seeing." Let's consider some thoughts about blindness and seeing.

## Five Narratives of Blindness

Do you know that there are five separate stories in the New Testament about the healing of blindness? The first and the longest of these accounts is found in chapter 9 of the Book of John.

> And as Jesus passed by, he saw a man which was blind from his birth.
>
> And his disciples asked him, saying, Master, who did sin, this man, or his parents, that he was born blind?
>
> Jesus answered, Neither hath this man sinned, nor his parents: but that the works of God should be made manifest in him.
>
> I must work the works of him that sent me, while it is day: the night cometh, when no man can work.
>
> As long as I am in the world, I am the light of the world.
>
> When he had thus spoken, he spat on the ground, and

made clay of the spittle, and he anointed the eyes of the blind man with the clay,

And said unto him, Go, wash in the pool of Siloam, (which is by interpretation, Sent.) He went his way therefore, and washed, and came seeing (vv. 1–7).

Now, following this miracle there were some rather extraordinary developments. The neighbors were confused by what had happened. Rather than rejoicing, some of them tried to explain it away by saying that the man claiming to be healed wasn't really the blind man but just someone who looked like him. The Pharisees questioned the man; and when they found that Jesus had mixed clay and spittle, they were critical because He hadn't kept the Sabbath day. They questioned the man's parents concerning who had done it and questioned the man himself. The man who had been healed then asked a very logical question: Why would God allow his power to be used by a man who is a sinner? The Pharisees had no answer except to say, in so many words, "How dare *you* a blind beggar disagree with us?" and they "cast him out" of the synagogue (see vv. 8–34).

Jesus heard that they had cast him out; and when he had found him, he said unto him, Dost thou believe on the Son of God?

He answered and said, Who is he, Lord, that I might believe on him?

And Jesus said unto him, Thou hast both seen him, and it is he that talketh with thee.

And he said, Lord, I believe. And he worshipped him. (vv. 35–38)

This story raises some interesting questions about who was really blind—the man who was healed or the neighbors and the Pharisees who refused to admit that a miracle had been performed.

The second story about blindness is found in Luke chapter 18.

And it came to pass, that as he was come nigh unto Jericho, a certain blind man sat by the way side begging:

And hearing the multitude pass by, he asked what it meant.

And they told him, that Jesus of Nazareth passeth by.

And he cried, saying, Jesus, thou Son of David, have mercy on me.

And they which went before rebuked him, that he should hold his peace: but he cried so much the more, Thou Son of David, have mercy on me.

And Jesus stood, and commanded him to be brought unto him: and when he was come near, he asked him,

Saying, What wilt thou that I shall do unto thee? And he said, Lord, that I may receive my sight.

And Jesus said unto him, Receive thy sight: thy faith hath saved thee.

And immediately he received his sight, and followed him, glorifying God: and all the people, when they saw it, gave praise unto God. (vv. 35–43)

This experience is interesting because of how Jesus honored the blind man's agency. He could have guessed what the man wanted, but instead he asked him, dealing with him in a way that retained his dignity and self-respect and telling him that it was his own faith that would make possible the restoration of his sight. This was not only an enlightening experience but an empowering experience for the blind man.

The third story involves two men and is recorded in Matthew, chapter 9:

And when Jesus departed thence, two blind men followed him, crying, and saying, Thou Son of David, have mercy on us.

And when he was come into the house, the blind men

came to him: and Jesus saith unto them, Believe ye that I am able to do this? They said unto him, Yea, Lord.

Then touched he their eyes, saying, According to your faith be it unto you.

And their eyes were opened. (vv. 27–30)

This account is interesting because Jesus does not respond immediately as he did in the first two stories. Instead, it's almost as if he's testing the faith of these men. He continues to walk and thus they have to choose whether to follow him along the road or to abandon their quest. They choose to follow him; and then, when he comes into his house, he asks them directly if they think he has the power to heal them. So both their behavior and their words must establish their faith in him. And then by the power of his word, he restores their sight to them.

The fourth incidence is recorded in Matthew chapter 20, and again involves two blind men:

And, behold, two blind men sitting by the way side, when they heard that Jesus passed by, cried out, saying, Have mercy on us, O Lord, thou Son of David.

And the multitude rebuked them, because they should hold their peace: but they cried the more, saying, Have mercy on us, O Lord, thou Son of David.

And Jesus stood still, and called them, and said, What will ye that I shall do unto you?

They say unto him, Lord, that our eyes may be opened.

So Jesus had compassion on them, and touched their eyes: and immediately their eyes received sight, and they followed him. (vv. 30–34)

This story has several elements of the others in it. They clamor determinedly to be heard, even when some people try to hush them. They plead for Jesus' mercy. Again, Jesus honors their agency by asking them to put into words the request that he could have guessed.

And, just as for the blind man in the first story, he touches their eyes and they immediately receive their sight.

The fifth story is in Mark chapter 8:

> And he cometh to Bethsaida; and they bring a blind man unto him, and besought him to touch him.
>
> And he took the blind man by the hand, and led him out of the town; and when he had spit on his eyes, and put his hands upon him, he asked him if he saw ought.
>
> And he looked up, and said, I see men as trees, walking.
>
> After that he put his hands again upon his eyes, and made him look up: and he was restored, and saw every man clearly. (vv. 22–26)

I wonder who the people were who brought the blind man to Jesus, and I wonder if the blind man was himself confused or doubting. I wonder why Jesus led him away from the town. I wonder if perhaps the blind man needed to walk with Jesus' hand holding his and with Jesus' voice in his ears so that faith could begin to build in his heart or perhaps so they could be away from the multitude, although the presence of others had not apparently been a problem in the other miracles. It's interesting, too, that Jesus applies spit to the man's eyes and *also* lays his hands upon him, and it's very interesting that the blind man at first is confused by what he sees and describes the men as looking like trees walking. This is the only miracle where Jesus lays hands on the recipient of the miracle a second time. In some of the narratives we've read earlier, he doesn't appear to have touched them at all. There are many questions we could ask about this narrative and many aspects of it that are not clear to us.

As I've thought about what lessons these five narratives can teach us, I've noticed the enormous creativity of Jesus. Certainly he understood how eyes worked and knew how to correct problems with optic nerves and such. We might be tempted to think that there is something routine about such healings. Yet in each of these cases,

Jesus did something different. I think there's a lesson here about diversity. Second, I've noticed how he responded to the faith of those who asked Jesus for help. And third, I've noticed that he responded in love.

I'd like to explore with you each of these ideas in a little more detail: diversity, faith, and love.

*Diversity*

I hope all of you have carefully read President James E. Faust's wonderful conference talk on diversity (see "Heirs to the Kingdom of God," *Ensign*, May 1995, 61–62). The talk was a reminder to us all to look on the heart, as Jesus did, and not on the outward appearance. President Faust talked about minorities who need to move outside their comfort zone of worshipping always with people just like themselves, and about majorities who, because they are a majority, may overlook those who feel shy or isolated. Don't you think, as I do, that there are times when each of us is a member of the minority and times when we belong to the majority? I think we need to be comfortable in both roles and very comfortable in crossing barriers just as fast as we can identify them, so that no one feels permanently excluded.

We can have unity in diversity in the Church when we are willing to follow the principles that the apostles describe: to love as members of the same family, to live in peace with each other, and to love God.

There are two stories that illustrate my point that righteous people can be very different from each other personality wise, with unexpected and delightful benefits. One story involves Elder Bruce R. McConkie and the other his wife, Amelia Smith McConkie.

During the time my husband, Ed, was the president of the Japan Okinawa Mission and I was serving as president of the mission auxiliaries, Elder McConkie, then a Seventy, and President Ezra Taft

Benson, who was then a member of the Quorum of the Twelve, were assigned to supervise the Asian missions. Before our mission, all Ed and I knew about Elder McConkie was his public image—that of very serious, solemn, intense person, and a man of great gospel learning. So we were scared to death of him on his first visit to our mission. What we were to learn was that Elder McConkie also had a terrific sense of humor.

I can't remember exactly how we broke the ice, but I think Ed must have done it. He just loved everybody and everybody just loved him back. A friend had given Ed a very irreverent present—a laughing bag. It was a gag item that looked like a little pillow; but when you pressed a button, it would set off a recording of someone laughing. Hearing it, people couldn't help laughing, too, first because they would be startled and second because the laughter was so infectious. For some reason, Ed sprang this laughing bag on Elder McConkie, and the apostle responded in the way everyone always did. He just broke up. He laughed until he had tears in his eyes.

Elder McConkie finally demanded, "Where did you get this? I've got to get one just like it! It's just what we need for some of those long, serious meetings!"

So Ed got him one! Now, I don't know that Elder McConkie ever took a laughing bag to quorum meetings. Somehow, I don't think he did. But sometimes I've imagined him sitting soberly in his chair with maybe a smile passing across his face at a moment when you'd have trouble finding anything to smile at in the meeting and know that he was thinking, "What this meeting needs is a good laughing bag!" Now that's a side of Elder McConkie that makes him a more diverse and interesting person—and not any less righteous!

And we also found Sister McConkie to be a dear and interesting and vibrant person. You might think, *Oh, she has nine children and she's the wife of an apostle and the daughter of a president of the Church. We know everything important there is to know about her.* That's what I thought when I first met her, when she was accompanying her husband on one of the tours of the missions.

We had a few minutes to shop one day, so we went into a store that sold pearl jewelry. They had some lovely pearl earrings for pierced ears, and I could see that Sister McConkie admired them. But that was during the 1960s when not too many women had pierced ears, and she said, "I don't know if we can buy these. I think the Church has a policy against them because it's cannibalistic to pierce your ears. But I don't know. I'll go home and ask my father." (I thought, *Lucky her! When she asks her father, she gets an answer from a prophet!*) Now, I'd never heard this policy, so I was very interested in what she found out. I was still wearing clip-on earrings—you know, the kind that make your ears hurt for hours after you take them off? And a few weeks later, I got a letter from her saying, "I talked to my dad, and he said it isn't cannibalistic to pierce your ears, so I got mine pierced right away and you can, too!"

Well, I immediately sent her a pair of the earrings she had admired; and when I got home from my mission, I had my own ears pierced. A few years ago, I saw Sister McConkie's photograph on the front cover of a magazine, and I noticed that she still had pierced ears. So that's another story about how interesting people can be in their diversity when you get to know them. Being the same is not at all a requirement of righteousness!

Dr. Victor Brown Jr., then director of Brigham Young University's Comprehensive Clinic and its Institute for Studies in Values and Human Behavior, wrote a wonderful article about diversity a few years ago. He said:

> Several recently activated brothers and sisters were asked to share their major problems regarding Church attendance. They all lived very close to the ward building. Among the fears that had kept them from attending were not knowing the right meeting time in the multi-ward building, where to send the children, correct dress, and the layout of the

building. They feared the embarrassment of being obviously different.

Think about the chapels you have seen. A characteristic of many Latter-day Saint buildings seems to be disguising the real entrance. . . . I recall that when we lived in Colorado, . . . a lovely curved walk with attractive hedges led up to an imposing door, which, embarrassed newcomers found out, opened into the back of the organ loft and storage room. "Veterans" used the little door back by the parking lot.[1]

In his article, Brother Brown included "a homey little list of some of the mechanisms which too many of us develop to either judge or exclude or simply take unnecessary notice of difference among us. You might add your own items to the list . . . [Ask yourself:]

Do I—

1. Notice the brand or quality of clothing of others?

2. Assume that [less-active] members are weak in all aspects of their lives?

3. Assume that active members are rigid and do not enjoy life?

4. Joke about others' grammatical errors?

5. Speak only with those who share my interests?

6. Keep track of those who bring their scriptures each Sunday?

7. Expect converts to adopt my ideas and ways of life?

8. Assume that lifelong members are less committed to the gospel than are converts?

9. Remember past sins and errors of members and their relatives?

10. Gossip about others?

11. Regularly ask, "What Church jobs do you have now?"

12. Lean up close to a blind person and speak loudly and slowly?

13. Comment on others' differences with remarks like, "Oh, what a cute accent," or "what lovely dark skin!"

14. Only have friends who are from my social or economic group?

15. Forbid my children to play with children of families who are [less active] but decent and honorable?

16. Avoid and criticize those with more money, better looks, and nicer clothes?

17. Treat people warmly until they begin to share their burdens, and then withdraw?

18. Avoid single, especially divorced, people?

19. Probe with questions like "What mission did you go to?" or "Why haven't you gone on a mission?" or "How many baptisms did you have?"

20. Probe with questions like "Why aren't you married yet?" or "Why haven't you had a baby yet?"

21. Fail to invite less active members to help the Church financially because I know they will be offended?

22. Hope Brother Jones heard the talk just given on humility because *he* surely needed it?

23. Judge other people by their children's behavior?

24. Know what the Lord means in Doctrine and Covenants 64:8–11?

25. Sniff subtly and move away from the obvious smoker seated next to me in Church?

26. Become impatient with older people?

27. Become impatient with younger people?

28. Spend a whole temple session wondering why a bishop gave a recommend to some shaggy-haired man?

29. Have a stereotypical image of lady missionaries?

30. Take it upon myself to warn newcomers about problem people in our ward?[2]

Does any of this sound familiar? And are there other secret criteria that you keep on a mental checklist of your own? If you have such a checklist, I hope that you'll rip it up into little tiny pieces and throw it into the air to become confetti for a party celebrating diversity!

Sister Barbara B. Smith, when she was general president of the Relief Society, wrote about the diversity of letters she received from women in many circumstances. They came, she said, from "women alone, women with children, women old, women young, women new to the Church, women in sorrow, women in despair, women happy.

"They form a mosaic of many lives with differing circumstances, with individual talents, and with gifts wonderfully varied. The details of each life are so numerous that we begin to see in them the great diversity among us, and with it great strength and enrichment.

"And from varied experiences comes one great unifying truth, echoing and re-echoing: 'I know God lives and loves *me*. His teachings make me strong and sustain my soul.'"[3]

When we are able to set aside the tendency to evaluate others and routinely identify the ways they differ from us, we are able to join the true fellowship of Saints, having hearts so similar that, as Paul said: "We, being many, are one body in Christ, and every one members one of another" (Romans 12:5).

To paraphrase what President Faust said, that unity of testimony is what gives us strength and lets us keep a healthy perspective on the diversity of our circumstances. We cannot be proud of our circumstances nor ashamed of them, only as they are opportunities to offer service to others.

*Faith*

Let's now consider a second idea: faith. Remember how many different ways the blind men expressed their faith in the Savior?

Sometimes he asked them directly and bluntly if they had faith to be healed. I think that sometimes we are confronted with similar, direct challenges to our faith. And sometimes I think the Savior takes us gently by the hand and leads us away from whatever constitutes our city, talking to us quietly until we learn to listen to his voice. And sometimes when his healing hands are upon us, we feel confused. We know things are changing, but we're not sure that we like what they're changing into. And patiently he continues to work with us until the confusion falls away and a glorious clarity fills our minds and our hearts.

Let me relate a time of miracles that was associated with our mission in Japan. Ed was called as president of the newly created Japan Okinawa Mission in 1968, just in time to get ready for the world's fair, scheduled to be held in two years, in Osaka, which was in our mission. The Church decided to make a Japanese version of the film *Man's Search for Happiness* for Expo '70, but they originally planned to film it in California. Ed wrote that it would be impossible to capture the spirit of Japan in California. Besides that, Japanese speakers in California wouldn't sound like native Japanese speakers, something that would be evident to Japanese fairgoers. After receiving these concerns, Church leaders were inspired to send the production crew to Japan to make the film. We were very happy about this, but we were also very concerned, because we knew there would be many, many problems to be solved.

For example, Scott Whitaker, who was the producer-director, said they would need a huge refrigerator in which to store the films. *How could that be possible?* I thought. Japanese refrigerators are very tiny, about a third the size of the usual American refrigerator. And of course, the American crew would also need a place to stay. There were only three of them—Robert Stum, the camera man, Brother Johnson, and Brother Whitaker, the director; but how could we ask them to stay in a Japanese-style apartment, sleeping on the floor on futons?

But the Lord provides the way. The principal of the school our sons were attending was planning to visit the United States and would be gone during the time of the filming. I called and asked, "Is it possible that we could rent your home?" He said, "That would be wonderful. We were just going to begin advertising for renters." They had an American-style refrigerator and American-style furniture. The home was also close to our house so we could pick Brother Whitaker and his team up and help them with any necessary arrangements and answer questions for them.

As we began looking for actors to play the husband and wife in the film, we had other problems. With the help of local members, we searched through many portfolios of Japanese actors and actresses, but many who looked as though they might be suitable had bad reputations or had appeared in pornographic films. Finally we found two men and a woman who fit the parts well and had good reputations. They could play the couple and the elderly grandfather. We also found children who could be in the family. The rest of the cast was made up from members of the Church.

One small miracle came when the crew went to Kyoto to shoot the scene where the husband looks into the water while he ponders eternal questions. It was very sunny, but when they were ready to shoot, it became cloudy. It became so dark they couldn't shoot the scene. The next day they came back. Again, the same thing happened. It was a sunny day; but as soon as they set up the cameras, the clouds drove in swiftly across the sun. They decided to change the location. Later they found out that at the very spot they were going to film, a well-known supernatural event had occurred in Japanese folklore, involving a statue that floated to the surface of the lake. The scene would have been widely recognized in Japan, and the associations with the native religion would have been confusing and inappropriate. Brother Whitaker said, "I can see why the Lord didn't want us to use it as a background for this part of the movie."

The Church hired the Takarazuka film crew to help in the

production and also used some of their equipment. In Japan, when a film is finished, there is traditionally a big party held with lots of drinking and feasting. When the members asked my husband if they would be having the celebration party, Ed said, "Of course." He was always ready for a party. The Japanese members warned, "Oh, when they have a party it means you have to serve drinks."

"Fine," said Ed. "We'll serve drinks."

Then he came to me and said, "How shall we arrange this party?"

I had a quick inspiration. I said, "We'll have a barbecue with American hamburgers, potato salad, potato chips, olives and pickles, all the fixings, and root beer." An American store in Kobe had everything we needed—right down to catsup and mustard. The film crew was simply delighted. It was the first time they'd eaten hamburgers and potato salad and root beer. You should have seen them eat! They had a wonderful time, nobody got drunk, and they said it was the best party they'd ever had to close a movie production.

Do you think that the Lord cares about the happiness of a film crew in Japan? Does he care about where a movie scene is filmed or about a refrigerator big enough to hold film for a BYU Motion Picture Studio? I can testify to you that he does. Our faith was answered. He honored our prayers.

And what is more, I know that he will hear and answer your prayers. Whatever burdens you are carrying, whatever spiritual blindness you are groping through, the Savior knows about it. He cares about you and loves you. And he will help you. If we need to be led gently away and if we need to have miracles come in stages so that we can get used to them a step at a time, that's all right. He is willing to do that for us.

*Love*

Do you recall the language of the fourth story: "So Jesus had compassion on them, and touched their eyes." As members of the

Church, we spend a lot of time in meetings, participating in lessons, going visiting teaching and home teaching, and participating in activities. But it is in our compassionate service that we are most like the Savior.

I was very touched to read a series of experiences reported by Sister Robin C. Beadles, Relief Society president, Lomas Ward, Mexico City, Mexico, that gave her some new insights into the concept of bringing sight to the sightless. To me, it epitomizes the power of love that our Church callings can invoke by giving us opportunities to serve. She wrote:

> Our family was one of very few American member families living in La Paz in 1987. Although I was struggling with the Spanish language, I welcomed the opportunity to serve as a visiting teacher in my ward.
>
> My companion, Sister Moreno, and I received the names of three inactive sisters to visit. Making appointments was a little difficult since none of these sisters had telephones. So, the best we could do was to make a "surprise" visit to each of them. We always said a word of prayer together before we started on our way.
>
> I must say that I was never quite the same after those very first visits that we made, as I had never before entered into such humble homes. . . . I swallowed hard and my eyes swelled with tears as I sat down on the small hard bed in the one-room home of Sister Salazar, the first sister on our list. The bed was the only piece of furniture in the room. She sat on one end of it and continued knitting. This was how she, alone, supported her family of five children, including twin baby girls who were just nine months old. The sweaters she knitted were beautiful and her nimble fingers worked quickly. The dirt floor was neatly swept. I noticed there was no water or electricity in the home. A small garden outside the door helped to provide for her family.

Sister Salazar seemed happy to see us and voiced her concerns openly. She wished she could find a better job that would bring in more money for her family. We could see that she was worried about many things. Her babies were thin and she was afraid that they weren't getting enough milk. Perhaps there was some powdered milk in the bishop's storehouse for them. We told her that we would ask the bishop. This pleased her very much. Because Sister Salazar had been inactive for some time, we invited her to come to church. . . . She . . . promised us she would be there with her family. She explained that she had not had visiting teachers for many years and thanked us warmly for our visit.

The milk was delivered the next day, and on Sunday we gave Sister Salazar a big abrazo (hug) as she entered the chapel. How clean and neat she and all of her family were! We felt so warm and happy that she had accepted our invitation. . . .

Months passed, and each month we made our visits to her home. Her family continued to attend church each week. . . . Our visit in November came toward the end of the month. Since I was returning to the United States . . . on the 5th of December, I explained that we would make our next visit on December 4th, which was just the following week.

It seemed to take Sister Salazar an awfully long time to get to the door that morning after we knocked. When she opened the door, I was shocked and horrified by . . . a grossly swollen and discolored eye. Sister Salazar's eye and forehead above had swollen to the size of a golf ball! It looked terribly painful. . . . Somehow an untreated eye infection had caused the awful pain and swelling.

"Have you been to the doctor? Are you taking any medication for this?" Sister Salazar very humbly replied that she had no money to seek medical attention. All that she had, she needed to feed her family.

I was very firm. . . . I asked her if she could come with me now. I had a car and could drive her to the hospital. I also had money . . . for her doctor bill. She was a bit hesitant, but almost relieved, I know. She knew she needed help. I made certain that she was given care, that she had the money she needed for the doctor, and also enough money to take the bus home afterward.

As I returned home myself that evening, I thought, "This is what visiting teaching is all about! . . . The first Sunday at church after . . . our vacation, Sister Salazar came running up to me and gave me the biggest hug and kiss. She said, "Gracias!" over and over again. . . . The doctor had told her that if she had not come in when she did, . . . [she] would have lost the sight in that eye completely. She did not know who else could have helped her in just the way that I did that day. A little visit, a little money, a little caring at just the right time had saved the sight of this good sister's eye. Sister Moreno and I had helped one who could have been physically blinded to see!

The second name on our visiting teaching list was Sister Amado. Once a very active member of the Church, this sister had actually served a temple mission in Lima, Peru. But since her return, she had chosen not to attend church because she had been offended and hurt by one of the . . . members. She had been spiritually blinded. . . .

Although Sister Amado graciously received us as visiting teachers, we could feel the bitterness and resentment that was trapped inside of her. [As] a widow, . . . she was lonely. Sometimes we would stay and talk for hours. However, she did not accept our challenge to return to church.

One month when we called on her, we found her . . . too weak to get out of bed. . . . Much to our surprise, [she asked us to arrange for her] . . . a priesthood blessing. As she recovered physically, she also seemed to recover spiritually. . . . She also opened up and told us how she had been offended years before. . . . I know that the Lord was with us as we answered her questions and talked with her. I felt that words were actually put in my mouth—even in the Spanish language! I was amazed at the scriptures that came to mind with the right answers for her. . . . The Spirit was so strong! It could not be kept from her! As we left that day, I knew that one who had once been spiritually blinded by offense and self-pity was beginning to open her eyes again. What a wonderful feeling to see Sister Amado sitting in sacrament meeting, participating in Sunday School and Relief Society. . . .

Sister Moreno and I still had one more sister whom we visited. We always wore sturdy shoes when we went to visit Sister Rivera. My four-wheel-drive vehicle only took us so far and then the hike began. The trail was usually muddy and steep. Sister Rivera's humble home was built right into the side of the mount.

This sister was actually physically blind. . . . She lived with some of her children and grandchildren. We didn't get to meet her face to face until after our fifth climb up the mountain. Only a little barefoot granddaughter would peek shyly out of the dark stone doorway. She would not say a word. She would simply take the flowers or loaf of bread that we had brought her grandmother and run inside.

We were very excited to finally be invited in one day to meet Sister Rivera. I think she really enjoyed our message and our visit. She never left us outside after that. . . . I knew that we could never bring sight to the mortal eyes of this dear sister, but her spiritual eyes were beginning to be opened again. Although we offered to take her to church, she felt that it was just too difficult for her. Nevertheless, I was always grateful that we could become good friends and that I could bring the light of the gospel . . . into her world of darkness.[4]

## Conclusion

Think how we began. First, think about the diversity that surrounds us in every ward and stake. Think about Elder McConkie and the laughing bag. Think about Sister McConkie and her pierced ears. Think about Brother Brown's checklist and, if you happen to be carrying around your own checklist, let it go into your mental wastebasket along with other trash you don't need. If Jesus Christ, the Lord of Miracles, never performs a healing twice the same way, perhaps we should ask ourselves how important it is to achieve mechanical perfection in any particular behavior or habit, too.

Second, think about the faith of those who were healed. Sometimes they already had great faith—enough to grope their way to the pool of Siloam and wash the mud from their eyes. And sometimes their faith needed to grow. We do not have to have perfect faith for a miracle. We just need to have enough faith to ask—for the Savior will always make up whatever we lack. Remember the American-style refrigerator that we needed for the Japanese version of *Man's Search for Happiness.* Remember the hamburgers and potato chips and pickles. And then remember that he cares just as much about the details of your life, and raise your voice from the roadside where you have sat in darkness, pleading for his mercy.

Third, think about the compassion Jesus had on the sightless and remember Sister Beadles and her selfless service to the Relief Society sisters in her stake. Think about President Gordon B. Hinckley's invitation to us all to do a little better, stand a little taller, and work a little harder.

This is an invitation I know you have already accepted because I know your works and your hearts. We are all human, and there are dark corners in all of our hearts and ways in which our eyes are all spiritually blind, but we worship a God of miracles. Jesus is walking along the road toward us. We can hear the sound of his voice even above the din of the multitude. And he will hear us when we call upon him for mercy and for healing.

Remember the assurance of Peter: "But ye are a chosen generation, a royal priesthood, an holy nation, a peculiar people; that ye should shew forth the praises of him who hath called you out of darkness into his marvellous light" (1 Peter 2:9).

May we always walk in that light.

# 3

## My Sister's Keeper

*I* invite you to consider the responsibility we have to be our sister's keeper. Sometimes I think we're a lot like children and all need a little help in understanding the concepts that Jesus tried to teach us. It reminds me of some children's descriptions of the Creation. Nine-year-old Bart confidently explained: "God made the moon and the light. Then the electric company took over, but that wasn't until many years later." Ten-year-old Heather remembered it differently: "In the beginning, God had some big ideas . . . One of them was round and had a lot of blue and green on it and some big humps called mountains." But perhaps Nancy, age eleven, said it best: "Love was created on the first day, and the rest is history."[1]

Sisters, we're part of that history that began with the creation of love, and being our sister's keeper is both a daunting challenge and a beautiful reward. I have three questions I'd like to explore with you: First, what is sisterhood? Second, how can we recognize and honor our diversity and still be a united sisterhood? And third, what opportunities and means do we have for cherishing each other?

### Sisterhood

Let's begin with the concept of sisterhood. Biological sisterhood is based, at the very minimum, on shared DNA from having at least one parent in common. Usually it's also based on having many years of experience in growing up together—sharing the same memories, knowing the same places, and interacting with each other in such ways as communicating with each other, serving each other, sacrificing for each other, discovering why it's not a good idea to fight with each other, and steadying each other as we pursue our separate but parallel paths.

I'm the only daughter in the Nishamura family, so I grew up without a biological sister; but I have seen my mother interacting with her two sisters. My mother had to drop out of grade school in the sixth grade to take care of these sisters after her own mother died, so she's always been "mother" as well as sister to them. And because I am the only daughter, she has always been "sister" as well as mother, to me. This year, she will be ninety-three, and she has been a widow for thirty-seven years. She had a hip replacement a few years ago and is getting a little forgetful, but she is otherwise in excellent health and enjoys life very much.

A few months ago, my mother, who lives with my brother and his family in California, came to visit me with her sister, my Auntie Shimeko, who is in her late eighties. She and Auntie Shimeko are both growing hard of hearing, and it was so comical to listen to them talking to each other, in both Japanese and English. Quite frequently, because they would mistake a word, they would answer questions that the other one hadn't asked. And then they would look at me and both of them would demand, "So, you are smiling! And just what is so funny?" And then we would all three laugh.

At night when they were both in the guest room, they would turn their hearing aids off. Then I would hear them both talking very loudly, both at the same time, without paying any attention to what the other one was trying to say, and I just couldn't help laughing again.

I usually manage to fit in a weekend visit to my mother, my brother, and my sister-in-law when I have business that takes me to California. Once I was able to arrange a whole week. And I was very interested to notice that, after I had been there for a day, my mother stopped treating me like a guest and immediately became my mother again, giving me orders and advice. Finally, I asked, "Mom, do you know how old I am?" She laughed and said, "Yes, I think I *do* know how old you are." Then the stream of advice stopped.

I took her shopping a couple of times because she loves new clothes and wanted to look stylish for a family wedding that was coming up. After she had chosen her dress, I surprised her with a matching pair of shoes, and she was as delighted as a girl.

These experiences are bonding. In addition to all of the years of growing up and the feelings of affection and respect we mutually share, there is also a strong feeling of comradeship in our on-going relationship.

In one respect, however, we have different experiences. I am the only Latter-day Saint in my family. My mother has been a Buddhist all her life, and as far as I know, all of the Nishimura family members have been Buddhists back to the sixth century when Buddhism reached Japan from China. Our differing religions are not a barrier between us because she respects Mormonism and I treasure and appreciate the good teachings that I received as a child from Buddhism. But our religions are also not a bond between us. It is my sisters in the gospel who provide sharing in this very important area of my life.

For example, one January I was in Alaska, where I spoke to five groups in Anchorage and Fairbanks—such a beautiful place! I laughed and laughed at that little sheet they gave me, introducing me to Alaskan culture. It read:

Going outside is not meaning simply going out the door.

The Lower 48 is not referring to that acreage on our farms.

Needing to jump the car is not a new weird Alaskan sport.

Dealing with permafrost is not the Alaskan woman's way of ignoring her freezer.

Forty below is not a sewing measurement.

Cheechako is not a half-hearted effort at saying Chieko.

My hostess in Fairbanks was Carolee Gho, an Eskimo woman who is married to a Chilean man. She and her husband are both converts. Sister Gho still lives a very traditional lifestyle. For Sunday dinner, we dined on a delicious roast from a moose that they had shot and dressed out themselves, homemade bread served with cranberries sweetened with banana, home-canned beans, and potatoes and carrots they had grown in their garden. Of all the items for the dinner, the grocery store had provided only the bananas and lettuce for a salad. She sent me home with salmon that she had caught and smoked herself and told me stories about growing fifty-four pound cabbages, one of the few vegetables that will mature in that short growing season. I was fascinated by the experiences she shared with me, and I had a true sisterly feeling for her, we two women there on the edge of the Arctic Circle.

Another weekend I was at a retreat for about five hundred LDS women in Florida, where we were able to share our convictions that Jesus Christ is the strength in our lives. As I caught glimpses into the lives of these women and as my soul was refreshed, my heart was filled with rejoicing and gratitude that these women stand beside me within the Church.

Then I visited some stakes in Michigan, where the sisters had prepared for the conference by sharing with each other and with me some memories and appreciations of Relief Society. Bernice Lonell of Troy Ward in Bloomfield Hills Stake captured beautifully the sense of sisterhood she experienced by writing:

> Having a common bond with so many women [in Relief Society] has been a blessing. It's not a bond of sewing and cooking, neither of which I do well. It's not a bond of personality similarities; we are all so different with different cultures and backgrounds. The bond is far deeper and greater . . . [one based upon] a desire to love all humankind, to serve one another and to serve God and become more Christlike. And the greatest bond I have felt is [our] . . . immense love for our children. . . . The desire for our children's righteousness, to turn their hearts toward Christ,

to attain the greatest joy and fulfillment of this life and the celestial kingdom has been one of my common threads to Relief Society.[2]

When we really see each other as individuals who are precious to the Savior and precious to each other, there is a common and precious bond. But given our shared beliefs in the gospel, why are there women who feel that they have no place in the Church?

I remember some time ago reading a story in the *Ensign.* It was supposed to be an inspirational story about reactivation—and in many ways, it was. It was written by a sister in California who told about a time in her life when she and her husband, Jim, were inactive. The bishop and the Regional Representative came to visit, and in a gesture of reconciliation warmly inquired about their circumstances and asked if there were a problem they could help resolve or if someone had offended them. Then she wrote:

> The bishop then asked the question that changed our life. "Is there any reason you can't come to church on Sunday?"
>
> Regarding each other for a moment, Jim and I knew there was only one honest answer. We turned to the bishop and shook our heads. "No."
>
> Our worries about being snubbed by ward members the next Sunday proved to be groundless. From the moment we entered the building, various ward members showered us with kind attentions. Their love helped us feel right at home.

So this is a success story, right? But at this point, I found myself wondering, "Why were Brother and Sister Ireland worried about being snubbed by the ward members? What in their experience warned them that this was even a possibility?" Then she continues:

> One Sunday soon after our return to church, Jim was out of town, so I attended church alone. The president of our

Sunday School class welcomed me and asked about Jim. I explained Jim's absence, adding, "But you don't have to worry about us coming to church—we're here to stay."

The good brother responded, "Oh, I wasn't worried about that. I just wanted to be sure Jim wasn't ill."

[She concludes:] A ward filled with dedicated Saints was there to welcome and to love, not to condemn or rebuff.[3]

So it really was a success story. I'm sure that's why the *Ensign* printed it. But there's a second story lying under the surface. We don't know how or why or from where Sister Ireland had learned the lesson that some wards had members that would snub them or be unkind. We don't know how or why or where she learned that she needed to justify her husband's absence and provide reassurances of their commitment. But somehow she *had* learned that. I'm so glad she was learning a different set of lessons at that point, but I wondered where she had learned the first set, and I wonder if some sisters in our wards now are learning, by listening to the talk in the halls or before lessons, that if they were to start missing meetings they would be gossiped about or immediately slip into a less desirable category.

Perhaps because of my background as a Japanese-American woman, I am very sensitive to thoughtless or careless or completely unintentional messages that set up barriers between people—and especially between women, since we can be marginalized so easily.

A single woman in Florida who was a convert to the Church felt marginalized as a single woman because in fairly obvious ways, she was not being treated as a full participant in the Church. She did not have home teachers for a long time, for instance, and though she would like to have helped, single women in her stake were not invited to offer the missionaries meals. Many single women in her position would have slipped quietly into inactivity. Instead, she found a very creative way to make a more secure place for herself and for women similar to her. She told me with real delight: "I was bold enough to go to the stand on a testimony Sunday and say that I was upset about not having the priesthood [holders] visit my home but I still believed that some day it would happen. As a result, several of us single women started getting visited."[4]

I think her message accomplished two goals simultaneously. First, it testified to her faith in the way things were *supposed* to work while making it clear that this wasn't the way things were currently working. And second, it obviously pricked an elders quorum president in his heart. It passed the two tests of "speaking the truth," not harshly but "in love" as the Apostle Paul counseled the Ephesian Saints to do (Ephesians 4:15).

Lorna Johanson, another of the Bloomfield Hills Stake Relief Society sisters, expressed a long history of interactions with many visiting teachers. Notice what these examples have in common:

As a child I recall the sweet visiting teacher who befriended my then-inactive mother and loved her and included her in her activities, never passing judgment. As a young newlywed, a number of sisters, knowing how desperately I longed for children, allowed me to share the joy of their own families. . . . Eventually we had four beautiful girls; and with each one, those early relationships have grown deeper and more appreciated. Then, a number of years ago, my husband lost his job; and again, there were sweet, loving Relief Society sisters to quietly render more Christlike service: a visiting teacher who took great care to make sure that our limited finances never excluded me from homemaking meeting, a dear friend who watched out for our well-being without ever threatening our dignity, and a wonderful visiting teaching partner who bought our Christmas tree toward the end of a year-long lay off. When my husband finally found a job, it was to bring us clear across the country from Seattle, where we'd lived for over twenty years, to Michigan. And again, the Relief Society was there with more examples of Christ and his love for each of us. The greatest personal example was one sister who also had moved from California at the same time that we had moved from Seattle. Rather than sitting back to let life come to her, she went and grabbed it—including me. What a blessing at a time when I thought I'd been forgotten. So it isn't just one event, lesson, or act of kindness or service that has been a constant example of Christ and his love. It has been a lifetime of quiet, simple, seemingly insignificant occurrences which have shown me that Christ is mindful of each of us and wants to provide ways to keep us close to him if we will only accept them.[5]

As Sister Johanson says, there was nothing spectacular in any of these examples. What's spectacular is the overall pattern of a lifetime. In each case, the underlying assumption of the relationship was, "What do you, as an individual, need right now?" And then the visiting teacher found a way to meet that need, whether it was in providing nonjudgmental inclusion, sharing a baby, or the giving of a Christmas tree. Lorna didn't mention what kind of friendship she offered as a visiting teacher; but if I were a gambling woman, I'd have no hesitation in betting that she's exactly this kind of visiting teacher herself.

## Diversity

We've discussed the way that sisterhood grows, even when it comes in small ways and even when it meets barriers. As Mormon women, our unity in the gospel is an unshakable foundation, but sometimes we mistakenly believe that the foundation is also the roof and the walls. I don't know about you, but, although I'm very grateful for the solid, impervious slabs of concrete that form the foundation of my house, I like wood and glass and stone in other parts. I want walls and windows and doorways. I want high ceilings in some places and low in others. I want stairs. I want hardwood floors, and tiled floors, and carpeted floors. I have a diversity of needs and that's why

I need a diversity of materials and spaces within my home. I think it's significant that Alma, teaching his people the gospel at the waters of Mormon, taught them to "walk uprightly before God, imparting to one another both temporally and spiritually according to their *needs* and their *wants*" (Mosiah 18:29; emphasis added). Sometimes we concentrate on needs to the extent that we communicate that all "wants" must be suppressed as superfluous luxuries. Well, the Lord seems to recognize and acknowledge our need for individual desires too.

But has it ever happened to you that you look around the Relief Society room and feel that you're only there because you managed to find a disguise that is fooling everyone else? Being excluded is painful, but even more painful is the feeling that you are accepted only because no one knows who you really are. Here's a little exercise to explore this topic of inclusion and exclusion.

When I was serving in the Relief Society general presidency, I received a copy of my first book, called *Lighten Up!* after it had been translated into German. The title came out to be *Nimm's Nicht So Schwer!* in German. In my portrait on the back cover, my complexion came out an appetizing golden brown, like a nicely cooked hotcake, and most disconcerting of all, I was identified as "Erste Ratgeberin." *Ratgeberin?* I almost stopped there. "Erste Ratgeberin in der Presidentschaft der Frauenhilfsvereinigung." While I was trying to figure out what it meant, a friend who speaks German but doesn't know much about Relief Society translated it for me as "women's help belonging thing." And another friend who doesn't speak German but who knows quite a bit about Relief Society said, "Help belonging thing? For women? Why, that's Relief Society!" And so it was.

I'm not making fun of German—well, maybe just a little—but it seems to me that a lot of women have as much trouble finding themselves in Relief Society as I did in being the "rat" something-or-other in a Frauenhilfsvereinigung.

Frauenhilfsvereinigung. Sisters, that's us! That's all of us. That's all of the women of the Church, and hooray for us. I want you to know that I've visited both Germany and German-speaking Switzerland two or three times, and the sisters there are exactly like us in their love for the Savior and for each other. I felt instantly at home. And you would have too.

I want to be sure that you understand exactly how I feel about diversity. I love differences. They make us interesting and challenging and delightful. What they don't make us is good or bad, and I think we forget that sometimes. And whenever we do, then any difference, no matter how small, can become an object for judgment and condemnation. Take, for instance, the simple matter of the love of children, which, as Bernice Lonell has pointed out, is one of the most important elements in the bonding that takes place among Relief Society sisters. (And of course, we all know that many women in the Church are not mothers, either because they are not married or because of fertility problems.) I do not believe that a woman without children is incomplete in some way any more than I believe that a woman with children is automatically fulfilled or is more righteous than another. Yet one mother of two children may judge the mother of six as environmentally irresponsible, while the mother of six is condemning the mother of two for being selfish and faithless.

And this is just one example. If *any* difference at all can be turned into an occasion for judgment, then what should we do? My solution is very simple. I wholeheartedly believe in the Savior's words: "Judge not, that ye be not judged" (Matthew 7:1).

The Savior informed Joseph Smith: "My disciples, in days of old, sought occasion against one another and forgave not one another in their hearts; and for this evil they were afflicted and sorely chastened" (D&C 64:8). This scripture goes on to explain the importance of forgiving trespasses—in other words, the disciples actually *had* committed wrongs against each other—but the Savior seems less concerned with the fault than with the fact that the disciples "sought occasion" to feel hard-hearted and judgmental toward each other. If He condemned that kind of behavior when someone had actually committed a wrong, then what must the Lord think of us who in our hearts judge others on the basis of such things as their marital status or number of children or the righteousness of their children or any other differences in our circumstances?

When we recognize a difference between ourselves and our lives and our choices and those of another woman, we do not need to say, "Hmm, who's right?—she or I? Is she better than I am? Is she worse than I am? Who is being righteous here?" No, all we need to do when we recognize the difference is simply to say, "This is a difference. That's interesting!" There are no "shoulds" or "oughts." There's just "interesting!" And that frees the other sister to look at your differences and say in turn, "*That's* interesting!"

Probably a great many of us would not be active members of the Church—I certainly would not be—if the racial and ethnic diversity we represent had to remain frightening and keep us strictly separated behind impervious walls. Consider these facts:

An American soldier wounded on a battlefield in the Far East owes his life to the Japanese scientist Kitasato, who isolated the bacillus of tetanus. A Russian soldier saved by a blood transfusion is indebted to Landsteiner, an Australian. A German is shielded from typhoid fever with the help of a Russian, Metchnikoff. A Dutch marine in the East Indies is protected from malaria because of the experiments of an Italian, Grassi; while a British aviator in North Africa escapes death from surgical infection because a Frenchman, Pasteur, and a German, Koch, elaborated a new technique.

In peace, as in war, we are beneficiaries of knowledge contributed by every nation in the world. Our children are guarded from diphtheria by what a Japanese and a German did; they are protected from smallpox by the work of an Englishman; they are saved from rabies because of a

Frenchman; they are cured of pellagra through the researches of an Austrian. From birth to death they are surrounded by an invisible host—the spirits of [those] who never thought in terms of flags or boundary lines and who never served a lesser loyalty than the welfare of [hu]mankind.[6]

Another contribution in the Michigan conference memories scrapbook was a page by Jewel Caulkins of the Southfield Ward with a few words written on it with great difficulty in pencil. I don't know Jewel or where she is from or her background, but Jewel blessed me greatly when she wrote:

> You are child God.
> Good Luck
> Have nice day.
> Many blessings to you.
> Blessings your family.
> . . . Thank you in church.
> Please we all
> Love you much.

I love Jewel Caulkins for the goodness of her heart and for her eager love that reached out toward me even in this form that was obviously unfamiliar and uncomfortable for her.

## Cherishing One Another

And this leads me to the third point. We've considered how we build sisterhood by recognizing our shared commonalities and celebrating diversity by recognizing differences without imposing judgment. Now let's think about the third point: cherishing each other. Joseph Fort Newton said, "People are lonely because they build walls instead of bridges."[7]

Think of Jewel. She was obviously among people who did not speak her language. Perhaps she had no family members near her.

Perhaps she had frightening moments when she tried to figure out American culture, American money, or American social cues that would let her know whether she was in danger. I don't know anything about Jewel except that she used the few English words she could command to bless me and make me feel cherished. And if Jewel can do that for me, then we can all cherish each other. Lucy Mack Smith, the mother of the Prophet Joseph Smith, expressed this comforting encouragement to the Relief Society sisters in Nauvoo: "We must cherish one another, watch over one another, comfort one another and gain instruction, that we may all sit down in heaven together."[8]

Cherishing each other makes differences precious to us, not distressing or offensive to us. Let me share with you the story of a woman who found that her ability to follow the Savior was limited by a trait she didn't like in herself. She writes:

> Through the years, I've struggled with a critical attitude. Almost without thinking, I find fault with the way the neighbors keep their yard or [the way] the politician expresses her views or [the way] the driver in front of me drives.
>
> I confessed this to a close friend who admitted she faces the same struggle but has found a helpful solution. "I turned every criticism into a prayer of intercession for the other person. That not only helps me stop when I start being critical, it turns a negative thought into a positive action."
>
> Her suggestion sounded simple enough, so I tried it for a few days, and it helped me, too.
>
> For example, when she found herself upset with the thoughtlessness of her teenage daughter's friend, she turned it to a prayer, "Lord, let someone today reflect Christ's thoughtfulness so clearly to her that she desires to be like that person." When she felt harsh feelings toward the politician she disagreed with, she prayed, "Lord, Your truth

is larger than my opinion. Give this leader discernment and a heart yearning to know Your truth." She prayed for the mail carrier when he arrived late and for noisy neighbors and inconsiderate drivers.

She concluded: "Prayer enlarges the heart until it is capable of containing God's gift of Himself," I once heard Mother Teresa say. I'm learning that "God's gift of Himself" squeezes most of the contempt and criticism out of my heart.[9]

Isn't this a wonderful concept? I'm afraid that when we find someone annoying us, we don't instinctively find ways to cherish them. Instead, we find reasons why we are justified in taking offense.

An unknown author has written:

A reporter once interviewed the famous contralto Marian Anderson and asked her to name the greatest moment of her life. The reporter knew she had many big moments from which to choose.

He expected her to name the private concert she gave at the White House for the Roosevelts and the King and Queen of England. He thought that she might name the night she received the $10,000 Bok Award as the person who had done the most for her hometown, Philadelphia.

Instead, Marian Anderson shocked him by responding quickly, "The greatest moment of my life was the day I went home and told my mother she wouldn't have to take in washing anymore."[10]

Did Marian Anderson's mother feel cherished? You bet she did!

Another woman said that her sister-in-law once asked her, "What absolutes do you believe in?" By which she meant, which principles do you think are true all of the time? This woman thought for a long time, and finally answered:

> Only one—
> "Charity never faileth."
> I've seen Truth hurt
> Religions kill
> And Laws protect the guilty
> But even though I've seen love spit at
> And warmth returned with ice
> I've never seen true kindness backfire
> In the giver's soul.[11]

My wonderful friend Mary Ellen Edmunds, who served with me on the Relief Society general board, has a motto she lives by: "Love everyone. And if you love someone who doesn't deserve it, God will certainly not be mad at you."[12]

Hannah Last Cornaby, one of our pioneer sisters of the last century, left in her biography a touching account of the importance of cherishing. The event took place during a time when there was an acute food shortage in the territory and she literally didn't have food for her children. She writes:

> One morning having, as usual, attended to family prayer, in which, with greater significance than is often used, we asked, "give us this day our daily bread;" and having eaten a rather scanty breakfast—every morsel we had in the house— Edith was wondering what we should have for dinner, and why Pa had not sent us some fish. I, too, was anxious, not having heard from Provo for some days; so, telling my darlings I would go and see if Sister Ellen Jackson (whose husband was also one of the fishing party) had heard any news, I started off. Sister Jackson had not heard from the fishery, but was quite cheerful; and telling me how well her garden was growing, added that the radishes were fit for use, and insisted that I must have some. It was good to see something to eat; and, quite pleased, I bade her good morning.

I passed on my way the house of Brother Charles Gray, and Sister Gray asked me where I had got such fine radishes. I told her, and offered to divide them with her, to which she agreed, providing I would take in exchange some lettuce and cress, of which she had plenty. She filled a pan with these; and I hurried away thinking how pleased my children would be, if only we had bread to eat with them.

As I passed Brother Simon Baker's house, Sister Baker saw me, and invited me in. I told her I had left my children and could not stop long. She then asked me where I had got such nice green stuff, and when I told her, and offered her some, she replied, "If I could exchange some for butter, I would be glad." She then gave me a piece of nice fresh butter, which had just come from their dairy on the Jordan; and also a large slice of cheese. If I only had bread, I thought, how good these would be! Just then my eyes rested upon a large vessel full of broken bread. Sister Baker, seeing I had noticed it, told me its history. It had been sent the day before, in a sack, to the canyon where her husband had a number of men working. On the way it had fallen from the wagon and been crushed under the wheel. She did not know what to do with it, remarking that she would offer me some of it but feared I would feel insulted, although she assured me it was perfectly clean. I accepted her offer, and, after filling a large pan, she sent her daughter home with me to carry it.

The children were watching for my return; and when they saw the bread, they clapped their hands with delight. Bread, butter, cheese, radishes, lettuce, and cress! What a dinner we had that day! Elijah never enjoyed the dinner the ravens brought him more than I did that meal; nor did he more fully understand that a kind Providence had furnished.[13]

That Providence was the kindness that existed in the hearts of all these neighbors.

I remember once when a kind act from a stranger made me feel cherished. I was supposed to speak at a devotional at the University of Utah institute of religion and got there in plenty of time; but the parking lot was absolutely full. I drove around and around, winding through the lanes of cars, getting more anxious and more frustrated as the minutes passed. Was I going to need to park illegally and then go into the institute and deliver a talk to the students about obedience to the gospel? It didn't seem like a very good idea.

Just at that moment, a young woman climbed out of her car and came toward me. I stopped and rolled my window down, and she said, "I've been studying in my car and I noticed that you've driven past several times. Are you waiting for a parking place?" I explained my problem and she immediately said, "You can have mine." Without another word, she got in her car and pulled away, before I could even ask her name. I barely got inside before the meeting began, but all of my frustration was gone because of this simple act of kindness on the part of a stranger.

## Conclusion

Well, think about where we began in this chapter. With God making something green and blue with big humps and inventing love and the rest is history but also about building bridges of love to create sisterhood and learning to rejoice in diversity and to cherish each other.

Think about my sense of affinity with Carolyn Gho, a native Alaskan woman living on the edge of the Arctic Circle, and with the sisters in Florida and the visiting teachers of Michigan. Think about Sister Ireland, who had to surmount worries about being snubbed or not included as she returned to activity in the Church. Think about the sister in Florida who found such a creative and nonchallenging way to ask that she and the other single sisters receive home teachers.

Then think about diversity and about my surprise to find that I was really the Erste Ratgeberin in the Frauenhilfsvereinigung. Let's remember not to judge, not to find occasion against one another, but instead to recognize differences merely as interesting, not as good or bad. Remember Jewel Caulkin's blessing to me and how cherished it made me feel. Think how free we will be to cherish each other when we can follow the example of the woman who learned to turn criticism into a prayer, and reflect on the kindness of the young woman at the University of Utah who gave me her parking space.

As we build bridges of love, remember that bridges take traffic both ways. We will give and receive love.

President Hinckley gave us another reason to build bridges of love when he said, "I have seen time and again that love of God can bridge the chasm of fear."[14] We live in a time when fear can easily separate us, then swamp us. Let us build bridges of love to each other across which not only our love but the Savior's love can freely pass.

# 4

## LIVING A FIRSTHAND LIFE

*I* invite you to consider a few definitions:

*Apology*—

A statement with the words "I'm sorry" in it, made by someone who is too honest to lie, too brave to make excuses, and too smart to try to blame it on the dog.

*Bedroom*—

A place where, if it has only one person in it, the person can't get to sleep because the pile of clothes on the chair looks like a multiple murderer with a chain saw, and if it has two or more people in it, they can't get to sleep because they keep each other awake, arguing over whether it looks more like a multiple murderer with a chain saw or an alien lizard-being with a disintegrator pistol.

*Excuse*—

(1) A very good reason why you did something you weren't supposed to do or didn't do something you were.

(2) A not so good reason, shouted from inside a locked bathroom.

*Game*—

An argument with rules.

*Imagination—*

Being able to think of things that haven't appeared on TV yet.

*Leader—*

The person who, when something goes wrong, has to decide who gets the blame.

*Truth—*

What really happened, more or less, with the part about the Martians knocking over the fishbowl with blasto rays left out.[1]

These definitions are fun and whimsical, even if they aren't exactly orthodox or comprehensive. What I hope to convey in this chapter is the "real" truth—about the wonderful, true news of the gospel of Jesus Christ. And I hope also that these thoughts will strengthen your conviction and testimony. So, if there's anything about Martians and blasto rays, you'll know you should leave out that part.

We hear a lot these days about homeland security. Our hearts go out to those serving in the armed forces, and to the men, women, and children who are in harm's way because of armed conflict. And the feeling that has grown stronger within me as time has passed is that no sword, no shield, can fully protect or defend us in these latter days, when the bomb that falls in your street may have been launched from a location hundreds of miles away or when the mere fact of being alive can make you the target of a heat-seeking missile. At this perilous time, then, the message by which Jesus empowered his chosen Twelve has never been more relevant: "Fear not them which kill the body, but are not able to kill the soul: but rather fear him which is able to destroy both soul and body in hell" (Matthew 10:28).

I am a person of peace, but I am definitely not saying that death is of only minor importance—especially not in the circumstances of anger and violence that Jesus suggests by speaking of killers. I think he was casting two extremes in the most vivid language possible, to make it memorable for his apostles and to encourage them to ask the question I'm asking you: Who is it who can destroy us both body and soul?

Who can take away our peace, not only in this life but in all eternity? Of course, it's the evil one, Satan—if we give him power over us. But how can we put on the whole armor of God so that we can live, even in difficult circumstances, with the peace of knowing that our eternal life with our Heavenly Father is sure? How can we be armored against the dangers of temptation?

When we try to answer this question for ourselves, and especially if we have responsibilities as parents or teachers for young people, we usually begin by making long lists of "do nots." But I would like you to consider a different approach: Live a primary, authentic, firsthand life. Don't live a secondhand life. If your strongest, deepest relationship is with the Savior, you will have a relationship of joy and peace in which there will be less and less room for doubt, discouragement, temptation, and selfishness.

But what does it mean—to live a "firsthand life"?

Let me suggest three cautions: First, don't live a secondhand life *intellectually.* Second, don't settle for secondhandedness in your *relationships.* And third, most importantly, don't live a secondhand life *spiritually.* Jesus put it this way: "I am come that they might have life, and that they might have it more abundantly" (John 10:10). I think that what he meant by this is that we are to be real, be authentic, and have integrity of heart, mind, and soul.

When Alma is trying to persuade the people that they have become mired in a substitute form of religion, he reminds them of how it felt to enjoy the influence of the Holy Ghost and then asks, "O then, is not this real? I say unto you, Yea, because it is light; and whatsoever is light, is good, because it is discernible, therefore ye must know that it is good" (Alma 32:35). A firsthand life is a real life. It is filled with light. It is filled with goodness. And most of all, it is "discernible." You can tell it from substitutes.

## Intellectually

Each of us plays many roles in life. We're sons and daughters. Almost all of us are siblings. Almost all of us are either employees or employers. Most will also have a calling in the Church. Some of us are also students. I was a teacher for twenty-three years and a school principal for another ten, which has given me some strong views about the urgency of not leading a secondhand life when it comes to our educations and our intellectual lives.

Whether you're in school now or whether you already have two or three degrees, you should, as a Latter-day Saint, be a lifelong learner. Whether you're taking a formal class or following events on the Discovery channel, you are in a setting where you can explore ideas, wrestle with them, turn them sideways, stretch them, and let them stretch you. Educationally, seize by the throat your opportunities to learn and try to understand an idea frontward and backward. Try to discover where it came from, whose mind or minds it originated in, what forces came together to generate that idea, what limitations the idea has because of the human limitations of those minds, and what applications you can give it now, standing in the first decade of the twenty-first century, that the original thinkers may not have known about.

When it comes to ideas, I've always enjoyed Wilson Mizner's credo. He said, "I respect faith, but doubt is what gets you an education."[2] It's crucially important to be able to turn a different idea around, examining it three-dimensionally, in the context of your own intellectual field and values system, cataloging the differences and noting the points of contrast but without bringing them into conflict until the process is complete. Reasonable, healthy, needed change cannot occur if we aren't willing to go through this process. If we hurry through the process, we may end up junking a very valuable idea without seeing its merit; or we may prematurely decide that our own system is flawed and throw out parts of it that we may later discover were not only bath water but the baby as well. I sometimes think that we Mormons, because we belong to the true church, sometimes are very dismissive of anything we don't remember hearing in seminary or Sunday School class. That's wrong. We should be the most intellectually alive and curious people on earth.

Do you remember how Jacob wrestled all night with the angel? Jacob would not let him go until the angel blessed him with a new name and called him a prince and promised him "power with God and with men" (Genesis 32:24–28). I think this story is a perfect metaphor of what it takes to get a real education. It wasn't easy getting what Jacob sought. He was all alone with no one to help him against this adversary. It was night. It was dark. It was scary. It took a long time. And it hurt (the angel even put Jacob's hip out of joint as they wrestled). But Jacob didn't give up and, at the end, he had his blessing. Well, whether as a student or as a self-propelled life-long learner, you're not alone. You have friends, colleagues, teachers, and fellow students engaged in the same struggle, sometimes with you, sometimes against you, but only you can truly get an education.

Another statement I've always enjoyed about education is a rather flamboyant one by British novelist Arnold Bennett. He said: "[An] . . . education cannot be handed out complete like a cake on a tray. It has to be fought for, intrigued for, conspired for, lied for, and sometimes simply stolen."[3] I'm not sure all of that's true, but what I like about Bennett's description is the sense of urgency and commitment it conveys. Here's a man who takes education *seriously*!

You have things to learn from almost everyone you encounter. Teachers are your partners in the educational enterprise. Laboratory equipment and libraries and the Internet and handbooks and instruction manuals and textbooks are your tools. They are all resources for you as you make your decisions about what you should learn and how you should learn it. What's more, all of you *are* teachers. What are you teaching those around you? I hope that one of the lessons is that same sense of lively intellectual curiosity and a willingness to wrestle with ideas, not the idea that you are the source of all knowledge, which you are graciously doling out to the less fortunate. Francis Bacon said, "Disciples . . . owe their [teachers] only a temporary belief, and a suspension of their own judgment till they be fully instructed; and not an absolute resignation nor perpetual captivity."[4]

So if the last thing you read carefully was the instruction manual for running your digital camera or iPod, let me encourage you to dive deep and swim far in the realms of learning that await you. Have a firsthand experience with education, not a secondhand one. Ask every question. Follow every line of inquiry. Let book lead you on to book. Even if questions seem to be leading you into unmapped country, follow them. If you are honest and if you never go anywhere where the Holy Ghost cannot go with you, have faith in the process that you will come out into a wonderful country. Acknowledge both your faith and your doubts. *Respect* both your faith and your doubts.

Remember that "a school is a building with four walls, and tomorrow inside."[5] This is *your* tomorrow. When you were in high school, you heard endless speeches about education as preparation for the rest of your life. Well, of course it was, but what a lot of people overlooked is that the high school experience was *also* your life. It wasn't just a dress rehearsal and then, when you graduated, you got to try the real thing. No, the months and years you spent in high school *were* your life, just as these months and years are *now* your life. And these months and years are the only ones you have right now. So have a primary, firsthand, authentic relationship with your education. Don't think someone else's thoughts, accept someone else's list of what you need to know, or set your own learning needs and learning style aside, thinking it doesn't matter. You're all you've got.

## Socially

The second thing I want to urge is for you to have firsthand relationships, not secondhand ones. Don't become emotional vampires, living off stories on television or in books. You women, if you're pretending to be Miss Spirituality at the stake fireside but really looking for Stud-Hombre Cybermuffin at the mall, you're living a secondhand life—never being who you really are and never letting anyone know who you really are. I don't know which situation is more tragic. That was an example about women, but you men know what you're doing that might be equivalent behavior.

Don't be afraid of making mistakes. It's been said, "The [person] who makes no mistakes does not usually make anything."[6] This is really true in relationships. Do you know that marriages can be annulled in the United States if one of the parties has misrepresented who he or she is? As a practical matter, this means that someone will say he's single when he's married, or lie about his wealth, or fail to disclose that he's got a life-threatening disease. But people conceal and misrepresent other things in a relationship too, out of fear that who they really are is so undesirable, so unappealing, that their only resource is to commit themselves to acting out a part twenty-four hours a day, seven days a week. Well, no matter how motivated you are, you just can't keep it up.

I've suggested that fear is a reason why people are willing to live secondhand lives in their relationships, trying to be who they think the other person wants them to be while the other person is trying to respond as he or she thinks that other person, who isn't really real, wants him or *her* to be. Can you see how confusing it is to live a secondhand life in relationships?

Have the courage to offer yourself honestly and sincerely for who you are, even if who you are has some limitations. This can be frightening, but there's no rule anywhere that says you can't sincerely and honestly offer your best self, your kindest self, your noblest self.

In addition to the risk of being rejected—and I admit that really exists—an authentic relationship may ultimately hurt you because it means that you have to engage people where they live their lives. That means pain. It also means complete joy, of course, but sometimes we concentrate on the joy and sort of slide over the pain. Oscar Wilde wrote:

> If a friend of mine . . . gave a feast, and did not invite me to it, I should not mind a bit. [Well, I actually think he would, but he's making a different point. It's this:] . . . But . . . if . . . a friend of mine had a sorrow and refused to allow me to share it, I should feel it most bitterly. If he shut the doors of the house of mourning against me, I would move back again and again and beg to be admitted, so that I might share in what I was entitled to share. If he thought me unworthy, unfit to weep with him, I should feel it as the most poignant humiliation, as the most terrible mode in which disgrace could be inflicted on me.[7]

Please consider what our baptismal covenant actually means—a promise to bear one another's burdens and to mourn with those that mourn and to comfort those that stand in need of comfort (see Mosiah 18:8–9). The burdens that we bear with and for others can weigh as heavy as the ones that we must carry for ourselves. But in my experience, the love and the joy that come from those shared hours of mutual burden and grief and need for comfort are sweeter than anything we can imagine this side of heaven.

President Spencer W. Kimball has warned that even within the Church we can end up playing secondhand roles because of our titles and callings that will prevent us from having firsthand relationships with each other. He said:

> Too often in the past, organizational lines in the Church have become walls that have kept us from reaching out to individuals as completely as we should. We will also find that as we become less concerned with getting organizational or

individual credit, we will become more concerned with serving the one whom we are charged to reach. We will also find
ourselves becoming less concerned with our organizational
identity and more concerned with our true and ultimate
identity as a son or daughter of our Father in Heaven, and
helping others to achieve the same sense of belonging. . . .
None of us should become so busy in our formal Church
assignments that there is no room left for quiet Christian
service to our neighbors.[8]

And I want to add just one more idea. We hear a lot—as well we
should—about the importance of families and of building strong
families. But the best way we can do that, in my opinion, is to build
ourselves as strong individuals. Let me tell you a story to illustrate
what I mean.

A Chicago bank once considered a young Bostonian for
employment and decided to check out his references, one of
whom was an officer at a Boston investment house. The
investment executive who responded to the request for a reference wrote that the young man's father was a Cabot, his
mother was a Lowell, in his background was a happy blend
of Saltonstalls, Peabodys, and other members of Boston's
finest families. The man gave his highest recommendation
without hesitation!

A few days later, the personnel manager of the Chicago
bank called the man who had sent the letter and said, "We'd
*really* like to have a work reference from you before we hire
this young man." The executive replied, "I told you all about
him. Didn't you receive my letter?"

The personnel manager replied, "Yes, but we are con-
templating using this young man for work, not for breeding
purposes."

[And the moral of this story is:] Your family tree may
provide solid roots from which you can grow, but you alone

are responsible for the fruit you produce in your life. Genuine purpose in life does not come because others set it up for you; it comes as you pursue what you desire to achieve and to be.[9]

## Spiritually

To this point, we've considered the importance of not living a secondhand life intellectually and not living a secondhand life in our relationships. The third and most important idea I want to share with you is to not live a secondhand life spiritually. You may think that your Sunday School teacher is the most spiritual person you know or your uncle and aunt who are serving a mission in Zimbabwe are ready to be translated. Well, that may be true, but you cannot enjoy a spiritual life of your own by trying to live according to their script.

We've already noted that Jesus declared: "And this is life eternal, that they might know thee the only true God, and Jesus Christ, whom thou hast sent" (John 17:3). We need to know him. Not *about* him. *Him.* Not things he's said or done. *Him.* Not things *other* people have said about him. *Him.*

We can't have a secondhand relationship with Christ. It's foolish even to try. We might, with enormous effort, fool our former missionary companion or Saturday night's date, or even, for a few minutes on a day when she's very distracted, our mom, but there's no way we can fool Jesus. He knows us. He knows all about us. He has known us forever. Do we really think we can impress him by pretending to be saintly? Do we really think there's any name we can drop that's going to impress him?

I feel certain that God is not shocked at our ignorance, not angry at our stupidity, and not embarrassed by our foolishness. His invitation is direct, urgent, promising: "If *any* of you lack wisdom, let him ask of God, that giveth to *all* [people] liberally, and upbraideth not; and it shall be given him" (James 1:5).

What a joy to be relieved of pretense and hypocrisy and all of the little games we play! The Savior, who knows us completely and expects better than our best from us, also loves us completely.

I can think of nothing more tragic than realizing at some moment in this life or the next that we cannot recognize the voice of the Savior because we have spent all of our time listening to secondhand voices: to the latest self-help guru on a talk show or to the latest popular speaker on the BYU channel. I don't mean to be critical. These people are wonderful and they do wonderful things, but do not ever mistake them for the Savior. Do not ever let their voice substitute for the voice of Jesus calling directly to you, or the still small voice whispering quietly but piercingly to your own soul. I love the promise given in the Book of Mormon: "And then at that day will they not rejoice and give praise unto their everlasting God, their rock and their salvation? Yea, at that day, will they not receive the strength and nourishment from the true vine? Yea, will they not come unto the true fold of God?" (1 Nephi 15:15).

The Book of Mormon does not use words like firsthand or secondhand. It doesn't have a vocabulary that includes words like "authenticity" or "reality." But what is it talking about when it holds up the image of the "everlasting God" whose promise of salvation is as unarguably real as a rock? What is the true vine? What is the true fold of God? How many metaphors has a prophet put in this single verse to urge us and plead with us to have a real relationship with the Savior, not a substitute or secondhand or phony one?

Let me share with you the experience of Anne Osborn, a highly respected physician with an international reputation in her specialty, which is diagnostic radiology. She is married to Elder Ronald E. Poelman, an emeritus member of the Seventy. Sister Poelman joined the Church as an adult, and she decided early that she would never disguise her membership in the Church and never apologize for her beliefs. As a result, most of the people she associates with, addresses at professional conferences, or meets as she travels around the world to professional seminars know that she is a Christian and a Mormon. She says this isn't always a comfortable situation to be in, but she never has to worry about what she told one person or what she told another person because she always tells everybody the exact same thing. In one of her books, she tells this story:

She was at a glamorous party of medical professionals in a major city in India, enjoying the glittering nighttime view on the balcony and eating fancy hors d'oeuvres when,

> Without warning one of my colleagues turned to me and asked, "Dr. Osborn, do you believe in God?"
>
> All conversation suddenly stopped.
>
> I swallowed hastily and answered without hesitation, "Yes. Absolutely."
>
> It may have been just my imagination, but in the semi-darkness I thought I saw looks of wistful envy on several faces.
>
> "How do you know? How can you really know God exists?" one asked somewhat anxiously.
>
> I have always thought that to one who believes, no proof is necessary, and to one who doesn't, none is sufficient. But I was searching for an answer that might be more helpful, something that would bridge the cultural gulf and differences in religious background that almost certainly lay between us.
>
> Finally I said: "I think the feeling that God exists comes from the accumulation of lots of different experiences. Small ones as well as big ones. For example, I believe that God hears—in fact, *has* heard—my personal, private prayers and has answered them on any number of occasions."
>
> "God has answered your prayers? What do you pray for?" another colleague inquired skeptically.
>
> "Oh, it varies. Sometimes I don't ask Him for anything at all; I just express gratitude for my blessings and opportunities. At other times, I've asked for help with very specific

decisions. Some are major, such as whether to become a Mormon, which job to take, and whether or not I should marry Ron." Those listeners who knew my husband from our previous visits to India smiled at the last choice and its obvious answer.

I continued, "I also pray about relatively small problems, like when I have the occasional really difficult diagnostic dilemma at the hospital. Perhaps it's something that I've never seen before, not in thousands and thousands of cases."

There were nods at that one. Everyone had been in similar situations.

"So what do you do?" another inquired. "How do you go about getting an answer for a particularly tough case?"

"I ask the Lord to help me notice the pertinent findings and perceive other, sometimes subtle, abnormalities that might provide a clue to the case. I often ask Him to help me recall having read about similar problems, even in an obscure journal article or case report that I may have seen years before. Most of the time it works."

"And if it doesn't?"

"Then I ask for the wisdom and inspiration to send the case to someone else who might know what it is and what to do about it. No one knows everything," I assured them.

The discussion was interrupted by a call from our host to come inside for dinner. I lingered behind on the balcony, reluctant to leave the intriguing conversation. Ravi Ramakantan, one of our best friends and a highly respected Hindu colleague, had been quietly observing the unusual interchange.

"Anne, they really love and respect you," he commented, to my embarrassment. "Who you are, what you think, and that you are comfortable with letting them know how you feel inside is really important to them. That someone like you is a 'believer' means something very special. It gives them—well, *hope*."

One of my husband's former business colleagues had once said something similar to him, remarking, "I don't believe what you believe. I don't think I could live as you do. But the fact that *you* believe and live right gives *me* hope."[10]

I would hope for you the courage of Anne Osborn Poelman in bearing her testimony and her consistency in nourishing her faith. She is someone who has a genuine, firsthand relationship with the Savior.

A testimony is a living, growing thing. You probably have parts of your testimony that are really firm and solid, while other parts feel tentative and shaky. That's okay. The quickest way to strangle our spiritual growth is to pretend that we know more than we do and believe more than we do. Speaking several years ago to the students at Brigham Young University, Elder Marion D. Hanks talked about what makes an authentic spiritual life. He asked:

> Do you dislike hypocrisy and cant? Do you appreciate integrity? Do you rejoice in somebody who has the backbone, in spite of pressure, to stand up and say it as it is? Do you like somebody who responds to pressure with vitality and honor?
>
> Think just a moment about the kind of religion [Jesus] taught and practiced. You may recall a time when someone asked him what is really important and he answered, to love God with everything you have, and to love your neighbor as yourself. And the man to whom he spoke said, "Yea, Lord, that's true," and repeated the words. He knew about loving God and loving brother. Since I have first read them I have been deeply moved by the Savior's response, "Thou art not far from the kingdom of God" (Mark 12:34).
>
> Jesus had the capacity to respond to those things that

matter most. I often think of what he said to the Pharisees, whom he called hypocrites. Do you remember?

"For ye pay tithe of mint and anise and cummin, and have omitted the weightier matters of the law, judgment, mercy, and faith: these ought ye to have done, and not to leave the other undone" (Matthew 23:23).

[Jesus] had breadth and scope; he had integrity and honesty. He had a great vision of the really weightier things; to treat each other with justice, with mercy, and to have this "faith unfeigned" of which Paul spoke. But these were not to be at the expense of obedience, for in this he believed also.

I love and have loved long [Jesus'] respect for honesty. Do you remember the day when a wonderful man, who didn't know all the answers, came to the Savior—having tried to get help from the apostles, who could not help him—to ask directly from this great godly one, the succor that he needed? He had a little boy who was sick. Do you know how that feels? This was an honest man who wanted desperately to get some help for his little boy, and who tried with the apostles who couldn't help him. I am interested in his response to that. He didn't curse God or [the apostles] and die, or go some other way. He somehow had a basic responsiveness and intuitive faith that made him seek the Savior and ask for help. You remember that conversation, I hope. Christ asked him if he believed all things are possible for him who believes and then the direct question, "Do you believe?" His answer? "Lord, I believe; *help thou mine unbelief*" (Mark 9:24; emphasis added).

Have you ever imagined how it would be to face the Savior and confess that there were lots of problems you didn't really understand—a lot of questions? [This man's] son's life and well-being were at stake, and he had the integrity to ask the Savior for help, professing and acknowledging that he did believe in the divinity, in his power, but pleading also, "help thou my unbelief." In the light of this incident, it has never seemed to me necessary to pretend to know everything.[11]

I don't know about you, but I've always thought of Elder Hanks as someone who actually does know quite a lot about the Savior. And for him to say that he's never thought it necessary to pretend to know more than he does about the most important knowledge we can have sets us a good example. We don't have to pretend to know everything. The Lord told the Saints of Joseph Smith's day that He "requireth the heart and a willing mind" (D&C 64:34). There's nothing he can't do with us if we give him our hearts and if our minds are humble and willing. And there's nothing he *can* do with us if we won't.

## Conclusion

Remember where we began? With bedrooms that neither one person nor two can get to sleep in because they don't know or can't agree on what that dark bumpy shape is by the dresser and about leadership and excuses and Martian blasto rays. I hope we've heard a little bit about the truth and have found a way to think about it as we live in a world full of risks and dangers. I hope that you can see a connection between putting on the full armor of Christ and what I have written about having a firsthand relationship with Christ. In that context, let's look at the separate parts of that armor. Paul tells us to:

Stand therefore, having your loins girt about with truth, and having on the breastplate of righteousness;

And your feet shod with the preparation of the gospel of peace;

Above all, taking the shield of faith, wherewith ye shall be able to quench all the fiery darts of the wicked.

And take the helmet of salvation, and the sword of the
Spirit, which is the word of God:

Praying always with all prayer and supplication in the
Spirit, and watching thereunto with all perseverance and
supplication for all saints. (Ephesians 6:14–18.)

What's on Paul's inventory of protection? Truth. Righteousness.
Peace. Faith. Salvation. And above all the Spirit. We can't pick up
the helmet of salvation on sale at Wal-Mart or inherit the sword of
the Spirit, which is the word of God, when we clean out our grandmother's attic. The shield of faith and the girdle of truth aren't hanging in a pawnshop, waiting for the first comer to redeem them. These
are qualities that we have to build into our own lives, day by day, in
the ways that we all know: praying daily; fasting in faith; reading the
scriptures with hunger and thirst; serving others selflessly; and
attending our meetings. But we need to do it, not with a focus on the
activities themselves or on our fears about the wicked world and how
we hope these activities will protect us, but with a wholehearted,
eye-single focus on longing and yearning to know the Savior. We
need to know him as our friend, as our Savior and Redeemer, as our
constant companion through the Holy Ghost. We need to know
him personally, know him directly, know him intimately and
authentically.

I hope these thoughts have created in you an increased appetite
to live an authentic, firsthand life. I hope that you want a firsthand
relationship with your own mind and heart as a lifelong learner, so
that you are not thinking anybody's thoughts but yours. I hope that
you want a firsthand relationship with friends and loved ones so that
the real you can meet the real them. And most especially, I pray that
you desire a real relationship with the Savior because that's what he
desires to have for you.

I testify that "the hour is coming, in the which all that are in the
graves shall hear [the] voice" of the Savior (John 5:28). We think of
death as the ultimate reality, but it is not so. The voice of Jesus will

penetrate even the mists of death, and it will awaken those who slumber in death. Those who have listened to his voice in this life will recognize it surely and awaken eagerly and to them will the promise be fulfilled:

> And the sheep hear his voice: and he calleth his own sheep by name, and leadeth them out.
>
> And when he putteth forth his own sheep, he goeth before them, and the sheep follow him: for they know his voice. (John 10:3–4.)

As the sheep of his fold, let us hear his voice. Let us follow as he leads.

# 5

# TURNING HEARTS TO THE FAMILY

*M*arriage and children and family life and homemaking are hard work. There are times when you will feel depleted, but the great thing about being a family is that you can lean on each other's strengths. There are times when you can provide strength to another, and times when you need strength from another. Both are honorable. Things become wrong and lopsided only when you refuse to give yourself permission to experience both the ups and the downs.

In beginning to explore this topic, let's first consider the concept of burnout. If you listen to all those talks on Mother's Day and Father's Day and believe all the articles written in magazines about parenting, you might get the idea that real parents aren't ever supposed to burn out, so most of us deny it when it happens. But, let's get real. We're only human, and you and I know there are cycles and rhythms and seasons in our lives. We don't need to keep on doing the same things or doing them in the same way. And we certainly don't need to do things in the same way as others. We can do them in our own way, at our own season. We don't need to force ourselves. We have seasons of strength and seasons when we need to renew ourselves in strength. Honor those seasons. My belief is that it's alright to cut yourself some slack.

We live in a time when controversy abounds, a day in which there isn't even agreement on what constitutes a family. So to begin, we need to define what the very term "family" means. So let's talk about what it means to be a real family in the real world today. Then we'll explore the need for integrity in our family and personal relationships. And finally we'll consider the need each of us has to have a personal, firsthand relationship with Christ.

**Defining Family**

There's a lively little Primary song that goes:

I love mother; she loves me.
We love daddy, yes sirree;
He loves us, and so you see,
We are a happy family.
(*Children's Songbook,* p. 198)

That's a definition that we can all relate to. Daddy, Mommy, children, and lots of love. The Church's *The Family: A Proclamation to the World* describes a beautiful ideal: a father and mother, who are united in love for each other and for their children, and we can add to that the expectations of temple marriage and activity in the Church and family home evening and all the rest of the pieces of that ideal model.

But do you want me to let you in on a little secret? The reason we need ideals is because we have to live in reality, and the reality is that almost none of us ever get to live completely ideal lives, no matter how much we want it and no matter how hard we work to achieve it. We live in a world where time and chance and forces beyond our control and the decisions of other people and even our own decisions bring consequences that we didn't foresee, all of them impacting and changing our lives. I love this ideal. It is right for the Church to hold it up before us. It is right for us to yearn for this ideal and plan for it and work hard for it.

But it is not right when we let the ideal turn to our condemnation. And the ideal becomes a condemnation whenever our real lives fail to match the ideal and we begin to feel we are not as good or not as loved or not as important to our Heavenly Father as others whose lives, we think, *do* match the ideals. Consider these circumstances that can make us feel that we have failed to measure up.

First, we don't get married on schedule, which, in our culture, is by about age twenty-five. My older son married at age forty-five. He earns a comfortable income as an attorney and is an extremely kind and compassionate person who donates lots of time to community organizations, maintains an active network of friends, and does quiet deeds of service that I find out about only by accident. He is also, in my opinion, quite good-looking. Furthermore, he lives in Salt Lake City, right in the heart of Zion. If you don't think he had some uncomfortable moments prior to his getting married, with people asking questions about his personal life, think again! Does this mean that he doesn't have a family or can't be part of a family? Not in my book it doesn't!

Second, suppose you get married on schedule but not in the temple? That happened to me. My husband, Ed, was not a member of the Church when we married, and some members of the Church said some very harsh things to me and about the quality of my faith. They didn't know that Ed as a Congregationalist was a better Christian than some of them would ever be and that I knew I could be a good Christian and a good member of the Church married to him even if he never joined the Church. As matters turned out, he was baptized ten months after we were married. He just took the goodness from the faith of his family into our new faith. We had forty-four years of a wonderful marriage in this life, and I'm looking forward to an eternity with him.

Third, suppose you get married on schedule and in the temple and are all ready for children, but the children don't come? Infertility is a problem for one couple out of ten, so it's not a remote possibility. Ed and I were able to have only two children, even though we would have welcomed a large family. Some probably wondered behind our backs why we didn't have more children.

Fourth, suppose you have children, but they aren't happy and healthy and cute babies who grow up to be bright, alert youngsters and turn into responsible, spiritual teenagers who happily go to seminary, love to save money for their missions, and who decorate their bedrooms with pictures of temples. Suppose they have serious physical problems or severe emotional problems? Suppose they drink and smoke? Suppose they use drugs? Suppose your son tells you that he and his girlfriend are expecting a baby? Suppose your daughter goes off for a weekend and comes back and says she's had an abortion? In our culture, what does this say about your family?

Fifth, what happens if your temple marriage unravels? If your spouse tells you the marriage just won't work because he or she is homosexual or has been having an affair with someone or has never loved you?

Sixth, what do you do if someone in your family is mentally ill? Or addicted to something really destructive like substance abuse or pornography or gambling? What if you discover that your husband or your grandfather or your sister-in-law has been sexually abusing your children? What if someone in your family commits suicide? Or is convicted of a crime?

The fact is, we don't think about things like this very often when we think about families. Instead we think of babies in hair ribbons and ice-cream cones and Scrabble games and bedtime stories.

So even if your mom sees to it that you're inoculated against every disease in the book, there is no way to be completely protected against the ills and trials and adversities of living in mortality.

Real families have real problems. Serious problems. Families comes in all shapes and sizes and configurations. But every family is precious. Every family needs support. In behavioral terms, it means that the casseroles should go to the family with the pregnant teenager as well as to the married mother who just had twins. It means that the divorced man or woman needs home teachers just as much (probably more) as the grandparents who just celebrated their fiftieth wedding anniversary. It means that the woman who just has been released from the psychiatric unit who raises her hand in Relief Society deserves to be listened to just as much as the bishop's wife. It means that the returned missionary dealing successfully with resisting same-sex attraction should be a welcome and accepted member of his elders quorum.

I don't think I'm going out very far on a limb to say that I know that you either have someone in your family with at least some of these problems or you know somebody who has some of the these problems. This is what real families deal with in the real world. And they don't stop being families.

A divorced family is not a broken family. It's a family with a particular set of circumstances that it needs to work with. A family with a gay child is not a failed family. It's a family with a member who needs special love and understanding and who has love and understanding to give back. A family with a pregnant teenager is not a dysfunctional family. It's a family with a complex set of decisions to make.

And I'll tell you another secret. This range of problems is what families have *always* dealt with. You may think that pioneer times were some kind of golden age without all the social ills that we face nowadays. It's not true. There was crime and illness and cruelty and wickedness then just as there is now. People were about as righteous as they made up their minds to be because temptation has always been available for those who are looking for it.

You've probably heard from teachers and parents that the world is a scary, dangerous, wicked place. That's true. You've heard President Gordon B. Hinckley counsel us to shun pornography and to study the scriptures and never to touch drugs or alcohol. I hope you obey him to the letter. It will eliminate problems you can't even imagine from your lives. But I also want to tell you that there has been significant progress in the world. In some ways, it's better now than it's ever been.

You will never know what it is like, for instance, to have *legal* racial segregation. You will encounter people who still believe that the color of their skin gives them a right to mistreat other people, but the laws of this country will not support them in it.

You girls will still find attitudes that will discourage you from getting a good education or using it after you've worked hard to acquire it, but you will never be turned down for school or most jobs just because you're a woman.

Fifty years ago, parents could beat children mercilessly and starve and torture them and it was called discipline. Husbands could and did beat wives. These things still happen, but we have names for it and laws against it and interventions to teach people a more effective way to behave.

Fifty years ago, polio was incurable. It crippled and killed thousands of children and adults every year. Smallpox and tuberculosis were major health problem in many countries, including the United States.

Fifty years ago, every country in South America had a military dictatorship. Nearly every county in Africa and Asia was controlled by a European government and was exploited for its natural resources.

Fifty years ago, smoking was thought to be the smart and sophisticated thing to do. There were dozens of songs and thousands of jokes based on the idea that it was comical to be drunk.

Fifty years ago, we had just pulled through the terribly costly and deadly Second World War. We still live with the threat of war, but most of you parents do not have to deal on a daily basis with the probability that your seventeen- and eighteen-year-old boys will be in armed combat.

No, nothing is perfect in our world, but there's a new sense of responsibility and compassion and respect for our planet and for each other that I'd say is progress. Just look at the number of temples under construction right this minute. Look at President Hinckley, going to places where no Church president has ever gone and finding thousands of members happy to welcome him. Look at the collapse of international communism and the dozens of nations that now accept and even welcome our missionaries. Don't spend one minute wishing for the past. There is plenty to be happy about with the world we live in.

And I'll tell you another secret—the good news secret, the best news of all. The gospel works like the very best kind of medicine. It's both a preventative and a remedy. It fortifies us and our families so that we can stay out of a lot of trouble by making Jesus Christ, our Savior, part of our family circle, and it also helps us get out of trouble by drawing on his matchless power and his boundless love. So let's consider how to do that.

## Integrity

I want to first call to your attention integrity. And the reason I think we need to start here is because we sometimes get the idea that if we can cover up our problems, then we don't really have problems. We worry about what people will think. We pull ourselves together and march into church wearing Sunday faces when the Saturday nights of our lives need serious repentance and the Monday mornings are times of pain and confusion. It has been my experience that we can't have good outsides, unless we start with good insides.

I want to make this point very clearly, so that you will not misunderstand. If you or someone in your family is being sexually, physically, or emotionally abused, you *must* stop it. You must protect yourself and the victim. You must get help for the perpetrator. You might think you are protecting your family by remaining silent. It isn't true. Abuse will destroy your family. It may even reach into the family you will someday establish and poison another generation as well. Please, talk to your stake president or your bishop. He will help you make it stop and see that you get the help you need to heal. If you are an adult survivor of childhood abuse, then you live daily with a burden that you need to quit carrying. If you are addicted to alcohol or drugs or pornography or gambling, you need help and you need it now. You will destroy yourself. You will hurt your family in ways that can't be healed for years. You cannot live the gospel with addictions.

What I'm contending is that you're going to have to choose between the Savior and some of these things. I want us to consider ourselves as whole Latter-day Saints—integrated Latter-day Saints, Latter-day Saints with integrity. All the parts and circumstances of our lives are valuable, important parts. We have been baptized. We have been confirmed. We have the gift of the Holy Ghost to tell us if some parts of our life are fitting together with the other parts to make a strong and beautiful whole. To have integrity, we need to learn to listen primarily to that voice, the voice of the Holy Ghost. Otherwise, we may find ourselves listening to two voices, trying to walk two divergent paths. Even people who love us may give us conflicting messages, because they see their path as the best one. Only your Heavenly Father knows the path you need to walk.

I want to illustrate this principle of integrity by a lovely retold folktale called "The Empty Pot."

> A long time ago in China there was a boy named Ping who loved flowers. Anything he planted burst into bloom. Up came flowers, bushes, and even big fruit trees, as if by magic!
>
> Everyone in the kingdom loved flowers, too.
>
> They planted them everywhere and the air smelled like perfume.
>
> The Emperor loved birds and animals, but flowers most of all, and he tended his own garden every day.
>
> But the Emperor was very old. He needed to choose a successor to the throne.
>
> Who would his successor be? And how would the

Emperor choose? Because the Emperor loved flowers so much, he decided to let the flowers choose.

The next day a proclamation was issued. All the children in the land were to come to the palace. There they would be given special flower seeds by the Emperor. "Whoever can show me their best in a year's time," he said, "will succeed me to the throne."

The news created great excitement throughout the land! Children from all over the country swarmed to the palace to get their flower seeds.

All the parents wanted their child to be chosen Emperor, and all the children hoped they would be chosen, too!

When Ping received his seed from the Emperor, he was the happiest child of all. He was sure he could grow the most beautiful flower.

Ping filled a flowerpot with rich soil. He planted the seed in it very carefully.

He watered it every day. He couldn't wait to see it sprout, grow, and blossom into a beautiful flower!

Day after day passed, but nothing grew in his pot.

Ping was very worried. He put new soil into a bigger pot. Then he transferred the seed into the rich black soil.

Another two months he waited. Still nothing happened.

By and by the whole year passed.

Spring came, and all the children put on their best clothes to greet the Emperor.

They rushed to the palace with their beautiful flowers, eagerly hoping to be chosen.

Ping was ashamed of his empty pot. He thought the other children would laugh at him because for once he couldn't get a flower to grow.

His clever friend ran by holding a great big plant. "Ping!" he said. "You're not really going to the Emperor with an empty pot, are you? Couldn't you grow a great big flower like mine?"

"I've grown lots of flowers better than yours," Ping said. "It's just this seed that won't grow."

Ping's father overheard this and said, "You did your best, and your best is good enough to present to the Emperor."

Holding the empty pot in his hands, Ping went straight away to the palace.

The Emperor was looking at the flowers slowly, one by one.

How beautiful all the flowers were!

But the Emperor was frowning and did not say a word.

Finally he came to Ping. Ping hung his head in shame, expecting to be punished.

The Emperor asked him, "Why did you bring an empty pot?"

Ping started to cry and replied, "I planted the seed you gave me and I watered it every day, but it didn't sprout. I put it in a better pot with better soil, but still it didn't sprout! I tended it all year long, but nothing grew. So today I had to bring an empty pot without a flower. It was the best I could do."

When the Emperor heard these words, a smile slowly spread over his face, and he put his arm around Ping. Then he exclaimed to one and all, "I have found him! I have found the one person worthy of being Emperor!

[To the other children he said:] "Where *you* got your seeds from, I do not know. For the seeds I gave you had all been cooked. So it was impossible for any of them to grow.

"I admire Ping's great courage to appear before me with the empty truth, and now I reward him with my entire kingdom and make him Emperor of all the land!"[1]

There are two lessons about integrity to be learned from Ping's story. First, he did not lie by commission—by substituting other seeds. Second, he did not lie by omission—by just staying away because he thought he had nothing to give to the emperor.

Let's examine the first kind of integrity—simple honesty. Think of the many pressures Ping faced to lie and substitute other seeds. He had to combat his own pride in being the best gardener. He had to combat his shame at growing nothing. He had to combat his ambition. He had to combat his fear of being punished. He had to combat his sadness at being mocked. The only support he received was from his father, who reminded him that his best was good enough for the emperor. Ping had integrity because being honest was more important to him than any of these other powerful, conflicting emotions.

There are many opportunities to demonstrate integrity, both in the Church and outside it. I love the story of Ping because it strengthens me. I am hoping all of us—men, women, and children—will be as courageous as Ping. Outside the Church we have many opportunities to testify of Christ and to behave like members of the Church in upholding the standards. When we refuse to compromise on the Word of Wisdom, for instance, we are behaving with integrity. The part of our life that honors the Word of Wisdom is integrated with the rest of our testimony of the gospel.

The second way in which Ping demonstrated integrity is that he took his empty pot to the palace, showed it to the Emperor, and told exactly what had happened. Sometimes this is a harder job than standing up for the truth when someone wants us to be dishonest because all they want us to do is to be silent, not to challenge someone else's reality.

Only a few months after I was called to the Relief Society general presidency, I learned a very important lesson from a brand-new General Authority from Latin America. We were reviewing a proposal for a video that was supposed to teach women how to be leaders in the Relief Society. Many people and many groups had reviewed this video. Nobody was completely satisfied with it, and we had a long discussion about it. This new General Authority listened to all of these comments and then, very simply and very humbly, he said, "I cannot see the sisters in my area in this video. The women in this video are rich. They have cars. They have living rooms with sofas and overstuffed chairs for their presidency meeting. They have manuals, handbooks, notebooks, scriptures, and pens and pencils. They have telephones. They are all wearing shoes. What is the message that my sisters will see in this video?"

We all instantly felt what he was saying. His sisters would not see how to run meetings; they would just see how they were not qualified to be Relief Society presidents because they were not rich like the American women in the training video.

I have thought many times of the courage demonstrated by that new General Authority. What if he had thought, "I'm new here. Surely my job is just to listen and learn. Surely all of these people have thought of all these considerations. I don't want to look stupid. I don't want to say that the women in my area are all poor."

This man was a good example for all of us. He didn't tell us what the decision should be. But he bravely shared what was in his heart. He explained very honestly how things looked from his perspective. He had the integrity to speak up when it would have been easy to remain silent.

I have thought of his example and that of Ping when I have been the only woman in meetings with men, or am the only non-Caucasian, or the only person born and reared outside Utah, or the only woman who has been a working mother. I have been in meetings and heard the teacher talk about families and divorce and children on drugs and how the gospel will solve all problems. Then I have looked around the room and seen women looking down with pain on their faces because they have these problems. I cannot remain silent.

In settings like this, I remind myself, *These men will not understand how a woman would feel about this unless I can tell them. These Utah people may not understand how a non-Caucasian will see this. This divorced sister may think she is the only person in the room whose marriage has ended if the teacher keeps on saying such things.* And that gives me the courage to share a perspective that nobody else in that meeting may have. I try to do it in a way that will not hurt or offend. I try to share and teach. Often the best way is by asking a question. Sometimes the teacher is grateful and sometimes not. But when I can share all of myself, when I do not need to keep part of myself silent, then I feel the strength of integrity.

You also have your callings and your responsibilities in which you must resist not only the temptation to be dishonest but also the temptation to be silent. Who will represent the point of view of people like you if you do not? Who will speak for your children if you do not? Who will speak for kindness and justice and mercy?

If the Spirit whispers that there are people who need to hear your voice, then try to find a way to speak—not to criticize or to force a different decision but to share your perspective. The Church needs to hear the voices of all its members—the voices of its women, its people of color, its new converts, its handicapped members, its divorced members, its teenagers and children, its mothers with small children, its priesthood leaders trying to help. It needs to hear from people who struggle with mental illness, with same-sex attraction, with poverty, and with sorrow.

It takes courage to tell the truth when dishonesty would be easier. It takes courage to speak when silence would be easier. Please remember that the Lord knows you, loves you, and calls you to act with integrity. Only individuals can have integrity. Groups can't—not even families, not even wards. The strength of your family, your school, your ward, your workplace lies in your individual integrity.

Now, as you've read some of these things, perhaps there are places where your conscience has pricked you. Perhaps there are times when you've allowed people to think that you agree with them because you didn't disagree. Or perhaps you saw somebody stereo-typing or marginalizing someone weaker and didn't defend that per-son. Or perhaps you heard gossip or an unkind joke and pretended not to hear because you didn't know what to say.

If you're feeling bad for any of these reasons, I want to congratu-late you because it means that you're repenting. And that's great! You can think about how you want to be different, and you *can* be different, starting now.

There's a third lesson about integrity from Ping's pot that I want to mention. Integrity is homegrown, and it takes time to develop. Ping spent a lot of time with his pot and with his father. He did not distract himself with video games or hanging out at the mall or tak-ing up stamp collecting. He was willing to stick with a very difficult and very painful process. I want to stress that. It was not fun or rewarding for him in the short term. It caused him worry and self-esteem problems and grief. But he stuck with it. And look at the payoff!

It needs to be stressed that the real payoff was not that the Emperor praised him publicly and the rest of his friends probably felt like eating the dirt they'd planted their phony seeds in. The real payoff was that Ping was a person with real internal strength. We don't know anything about Ping's family except what his father said. But where did his father's wisdom come from? Think about how values are transmitted from generation to generation. They're contagious, but the incubation period is usually quite lengthy.

May I invite you to think about the value of focusing as a family on a few very important projects that all of you can be involved in together and saying no to a whole lot of other things. Ping wasn't running a greenhouse or a plantation. He was working on one pot. By important projects, I don't mean just chores. I mean the kind of activity that says who you are as a family. Maybe it's a family busi-ness where the money goes into a savings account for missions and college. Maybe it's education in certain skills. Maybe it's the development of musical or dancing or athletic abilities. Rather than always choosing activities that fragment your family, pulling you off in different directions every night of the week and every weekend, consider choosing activities that you can do happily together with each other. And say no to the rest.

I'm not saying that everybody needs to do exactly the same thing. Of course people in a family will have different talents, different interests, and different hobbies. Also, people in a family need time alone and time with friends as well as time together. But put the family's needs first instead of second or third, and the solutions to some other problems will just fall into place.

## Firsthand Relationship

If we accept seriously our responsibility to think, speak, and act with integrity, we are in a position to draw great strength from our families and to give great strength back. Integrity is the foundation of personal righteousness.

I know you've heard this so often: develop a personal relationship with Christ. Well, how, exactly, do you do that? How does Christ become central in your life? How does he become a real person to you, one who is a powerful presence for good in your life?

Begin with my testimony that Jesus wants you. I know that he knows you and that he loves you. And he wants you to know him and love him, face to face, heart to heart, as a person. He wants to have a firsthand relationship with you.

But do you know what's going to stand in your way? Not sin or even laziness, although those two speed bumps are both perennial problems. The real problem is that it's so easy to have a *secondhand* experience with the Savior. We read the scriptures—because they're his words. We read books by General Authorities and other good authors because they talk about him and explain the gospel and offer their own witness of Christ. We attend meetings and listen to the testimonies of others. We obey the commandments. We retain our worthiness for our temple recommends. We serve diligently in our Church callings.

All of these are good things. They're not bad things. But they can be substitutes for better things. We need to know *Jesus*, not just know *about* Jesus. We need knowledge of the Savior, we need a clear intellectual understanding of the principles of his gospel, and we need to spend time with other good Christians, both to serve them and to be served by them. But we also need to spend time with Christ. He needs to be a face in our minds and a feeling in our hearts, not just a picture on the wall and a list of scriptures hanging on the refrigerator.

In 2 Nephi 25, where Nephi explains the grace of Christ, he also talks about how he achieves his personal focus on Christ. He believes in Christ, he keeps the law of Moses, he looks forward "with stead-fastness unto Christ," he anticipates the time when he will be made "alive in Christ," he talks of Christ, he rejoices in Christ, he preaches of Christ, he prophesies of Christ, and he writes according to his prophecies (see vv. 23–24). In other words, Christ is someone he knows, loves, thinks about, ponders on, communes with, shapes his life according to, rejoices in, and worships as his Savior. When we hunger and thirst for the presence of Christ, when we shape our hearts to his law and our behavior to this extent, then I think our holiness will increase and we will never need to take our spiritual pulse to see how it's working.

Let me give you an example. A few years ago, my son Ken came with me to Hawaii. We went to the big island and visited the little village of Hoea where I was born, which is now just part of the sugarcane plantation, and the only slightly larger village of Mahukona, where I spent my childhood.

I showed Ken the beginner's pool in the ocean where my father had positioned large rocks to act as a breakwater for us while we were learning to swim, and the big flat rock that we would lie on when we got cold and let the heat from the sun and the heat from the rock make us toasty warm again. We walked over the site of the house I had lived in. Nothing is left but the concrete foundation. I described the rooms and walked through them in my memory, and he walked through them in his imagination. Ken had grown up in Denver, Osaka, and Salt Lake City, and he served his mission in the giant cities of Brazil, so I could see him trying to imagine what it would have been like to live in a place with no electricity, no paved roads, and no telephone.

Inside the square outlined by the foundation, we made an exciting discovery—many chipped and broken dishes and broken glasses. I think my mother must have thrown these things under the house to get them out of the way so that we children wouldn't cut ourselves. Weekly garbage collection was another luxury we didn't have!

Ken got very interested and rummaged around in the space of the foundation, digging away the dirt and shoving the plants aside with his hands until he found a plate and a saucer. Each of them had a nick out of them, or a big chip gone, but he didn't care. He was delighted when he found an unbroken brown glass Clorox bottle. Who remembers when Clorox used to come in brown glass jugs? Well, Ken just barely did; but it was the association with Mahukona that he wanted. The discarded crockery that my mother had thrown away as useless, he fussed over, packing it carefully in his suitcase, so that it would reach home without further damage.

Now, I have wonderful memories of growing up on the planta-tion, but I don't feel sentimental at all about it. It was a lot of hard work. My father was a welder, among other things, and he put in very long hours. My mother had to keep house and raise us children in a little colony of about fourteen Japanese families, half a day's journey from a city of any size, and take care of my father's parents in addition. We were always temporary workers, always visitors on the haole plantation. I had a firsthand relationship to that life; and while it had happy associations for me, I didn't desire to reproduce it.

But I could tell that Ken, an attorney who works with his mind rather than with his hands, wanted a connection to it. He wanted to understand what it had been like there, to be in a place where the most exciting event was the visit of the grocer's truck once a week and where ice cream was a delicacy that we could have only every few months. He wanted to understand something about his heritage as the grandson of a Japanese laborer, and that imperfect cup and saucer were reminders to him, perhaps, that life can be fragile, imperfect, but never useless. That brown Clorox jug is part of my grandson's inheritance.

But Ken's connection and his son, Kenzo's, connection to that plantation life will always be secondhand. Ken can try to imagine what it was like, he can cherish souvenirs of that past, and he can walk over the ground and listen to my stories. But he can never experience it for himself. I had the firsthand relationship to it. Ken has only a secondhand relationship to it.

But it's not that way with the gospel and with a knowledge of the Savior. Through the miracle of the Savior's divinity, we can each know him intimately, draw upon his strength and power, and receive his complete love. Listen to these scriptural promises, phrased so that they have particular application to all of us, both men and women:

The Lord told Joseph Smith: "Verily, . . . It shall come to pass that every soul who forsaketh his [or her] sins and cometh unto me, and calleth on my name, and obeyeth my voice, and keepeth my commandments, shall see my face and know that I am" (D&C 93:1).

A second modern revelation to Joseph Smith promises: "And he [or she] that receiveth me receiveth my Father; And he [or she] that receiveth my Father receiveth my Father's kingdom; therefore all that my Father hath shall be given unto him or [her]" (D&C 84:37–38). We struggle with the arithmetic of this. If you give someone "all" of anything, how can there be anything left over to give "all" to a second person?

"Behold, I stand at the door, and knock," the Savior told his beloved apostle John. "If any [one will] hear my voice, and open the door, I will come in to him, and will sup with him, and he with me. To him that overcometh will I grant to sit with me in my throne, even as I also overcame, and am set down with my Father in his throne" (Revelation 3:20–21).

How is it possible for everyone who is invited to sup with the Savior and to sit with him on his throne? In mortal terms it would be impossible. A person can be in only one place at a time, and even the most spacious throne will eventually be filled. But in the eternal world, Jesus can bestow his company on each one who truly desires it and who overcomes the world. He has room for everyone in his heart. No one who is truly righteous will be left out. Each of us will inherit the fullness of the Father. It is a promise we can trust.

And ultimately, the strength in our families will come from our individual, firsthand, unique personal relationships with Jesus Christ. Whatever he lays his hand on will live. As he raised the daughter of Jairus from death and interrupted the funeral process to restore the son of the widow of Nain to his mother, he can heal and restore and nurture anything in your family that is marred and scarred. He can mend broken marriages and broken hearts. He can purify addictions and soak the stains of sin out of your soul. He can teach you how to replace harshness with kindness and silence with sharing. He can help your family have life and have it more abundantly.

And so I conclude, don't be afraid to yearn for the presence of Christ. It is his influence for which we hunger, his Spirit for which we thirst, his face we joyously seek. And we can trust his promise that he will be there.

## Conclusion

Let's briefly review where we've been. We've reviewed families and how every family deserves support and every family is precious.

Then we considered integrity and Ping's pot and the importance of telling the truth, both in what we say and also in speaking up when to remain silent is to allow a wrong to continue. We also explored the importance of saying yes to our families by saying no to other things.

In this regard, two of the most beautiful promises and commendations that I think could be bestowed on anyone are the Lord's praise of two men as recorded in the Doctrine and Covenants. He said:

> Verily I say unto you, blessed is my servant Hyrum Smith; for I, the Lord, love him because of the integrity of his heart, and because he loveth that which is right before me. (D&C 124:15.)
>
> And again, verily I say unto you, my servant George Miller is without guile; he may be trusted because of the integrity of his heart; and for the love which he has to my testimony I, the Lord, love him. (D&C 124:20.)

Sometimes, when the pressures are great upon us, both in the world, in our families, and in our wards, to compromise our integrity, remember Ping's pot. We serve not an emperor but the Lord of heaven and earth. He loves us for who we are. Our best is good enough for him.

And last, we reflected on the power of having a firsthand relationship with the Savior. Remember Ken, digging up the chipped cup and saucer from the foundation of his grandparents' house and letting these objects tell him something about a lifestyle that he can never understand except as an imaginative reconstruction. The miracle of the gospel is that Jesus Christ, our Savior, atoned for each one of us, not just for Peter, James, and John. He knows your name, just as he knew the names of Mary, Martha, and Lazarus. We can know him, think about him, talk with him, feel his spirit, and yearn to see his face.

# 6

# "A More Excellent Way"

$\mathcal{I}$t was quite a milestone for me in 2006 when I turned eighty, so I'd like to share with you some of the lessons of age. One seventy-two-year-old, when asked what lesson she'd learned, said, "I've learned that you should never take out your teeth when flushing the [toilet.]"[1]

Malcolm Forbes's words of wisdom were, "As you get older, don't slow down. Speed up. There's less time left."[2]

Bob Hope's wise observation was, "You know you're getting old when the candles cost more than the cake."[3]

And here's the bit of wisdom I like best, "Never let what you cannot do interfere with what you *can* do."[4]

These wise concepts seem particularly appropriate in light of the inspiring and challenging statement in Ether 12:11: "Wherefore, by faith was the law of Moses given. But in the gift of his Son hath God prepared a more excellent way; and it is by faith that it hath been fulfilled." It is the concept of the more excellent way that I wish to discuss.

What is meant by "a more excellent way"? During his mortal ministry Jesus declared that he had come to fulfill the law of the Old Testament and to bring a new law and covenant. His life, his teachings, and his example all pointed to a more excellent way—to the Jews of his time and to us, his brothers and sisters of all time.

This is the same question that the Apostle Thomas, "Doubting

Thomas," asked Jesus when the Savior gently told his apostles that he was going away. "Lord," said the troubled Thomas, "we know not whither thou goest; and how can we know the way?" Then Jesus gave him this beautiful answer, "*I* am the way, the truth, and the life" (John 14:4–6; emphasis added).

I testify that Jesus is the more excellent way. We know there are people who would willingly cooperate with Satan and with others to deceive many. But the voice of the scriptures, even its warning voice, is not to teach us to fear but rather to trust. We can trust the Savior. We can trust the truth. We can trust that, even though we are weak and struggle with many problems, our desires for righteousness and our righteous works, limited though they may be, do in fact lead us on the road to Christ. And on that road, we are not alone. We have the company of the Savior, the gift of the Holy Ghost, the companionship of other righteous brothers and sisters in the gospel, and also the support and help of those who are seeking for the truth, even if they do not yet know where to find it.

I want to share with you two pairs of gifts from that more excellent way. The first set of gifts comes from the Savior. The second set are gifts that, thanks to the Savior, we can give to others. But all four of them are more excellent because they are the Savior's own way.

I'll focus first on the two gifts from the Savior—his mercy and his abundant love. Then we'll consider the two gifts we can give to others—first, the gift of withholding judgment, and second, the gift of offering compassionate service.

## The Savior's Mercy

The most important strength we can have during mortality is our testimony of the Savior—our knowledge that he really exists, that he is our Savior and Redeemer, that he really loves each of us individually, and that he chose to experience mortality so that he can be beside us in our own struggles during this life. Think of how completely we rely, not on the Savior's justice or even on his love, but on his mercy.

It is encouraging to think of how many miracles Jesus performed in response to someone appealing to his mercy. There were the two blind men who followed him, crying, "Thou Son of David, have mercy on us" and, a few chapters later, the two blind men sitting by the wayside, who heard that Jesus was passing by and cried out, saying, "Have mercy on us, O Lord, thou Son of David" (Matthew 9:27; 20:30). Blind Bartimaeus, begging by the Jericho highway, received the greatest gift in his life when he cried out, "Jesus, thou Son of David, have mercy on me" (Mark 10:46–47). And ten lepers were made clean when they stood far off and said, "Jesus, Master, have mercy on us" (Luke 17:12–13).

Christ also healed the daughter of the Canaanite woman, in response to her saying, "Have mercy on me, O Lord, thou Son of David" (Matthew 15:22). And he granted the request of the father who knelt before him, pleading on behalf of his son, who was possessed and often fell into the fire and water, when the father pleaded, "Lord, have mercy on my son" (Matthew 17:14–15).

When the scribes and Pharisees were shocked and disapproving that Jesus would share a meal with publicans, he rebuked them: "I will have mercy, . . . for I am not come to call the righteous, but sinners to repentance" (Matthew 9:12–13). On another occasion, he rebuked the scribes and Pharisees as "hypocrites," reprimanding them, "Ye pay tithe of mint and anise and cummin, and have omitted the weightier matters of the law, judgment, mercy, and faith: these ought ye to have done, and not to leave the other undone" (Matthew 23:23). It was mercy they were lacking.

No wonder that the Psalmist wrote a great hymn to mercy that is part prayer and part rejoicing. It reads:

> Be merciful unto me, O God, be merciful unto me: for
> my soul trusteth in thee: yea, in the shadow of thy wings will
> I make my refuge, until these calamities be overpast.

> I will cry unto God most high; unto God that performeth all things for me.
>
> He shall send from heaven, and save me from the reproach of him that would swallow me up. . . . God shall send forth his mercy and his truth. . . .
>
> I will praise thee, O Lord, among the people: I will sing unto thee among the nations.
>
> For thy mercy is great unto the heavens, and thy truth unto the clouds. (Psalm 57:1–3, 9–10.)

There is a very striking story about the abundance and power of love, which Elder George F. Richards, the father of Elder LeGrand Richards, published in the *Improvement Era* in 1946. That was more than sixty years ago, the year after World War II had ended with its terrible devastation and loss of life. Elder Richards was known as a very merciful and loving man, remarkably so, even among the apostles. He reported that he had had a dream, just before the end of the war, in which he and some of his associates were in a courtyard where German soldiers led by Adolf Hitler were preparing weapons for an execution or a slaughter of some kind. Then a circle was formed, with Hitler and his men on the inside facing inward. Elder Richards dreamed he stepped inside the circle, faced Hitler, and spoke to him:

> "I am your brother. You are my brother. In our heavenly home we lived together in love and peace. Why can we not so live here on the earth?"
>
> And it seemed to me that I felt in myself, welling up in my soul, a love for that man, and I could feel that he was having the same experience, and presently he arose, and we embraced each other and kissed each other, a kiss of affection.
>
> Then the scene changed so that our group was within the circle, and he and his group were on the outside, and

when he came around to where I was standing, he stepped
inside the circle and embraced me again, with a kiss of
affection.

I think the Lord gave me that dream. Why should I
dream of this man, one of the greatest enemies of mankind,
and one of the wickedest, but that the Lord should teach me
that I must love my enemies, and I must love the wicked as
well as the good?

Now, who is there in this wide world that I could not
love under those conditions, if I could only continue to feel
as I felt then?[5]

Elder Richards's point was not that *he* was such a merciful and
loving person. His point was that *Jesus* is so loving and merciful that
even a Hitler did not stand outside his reach and that Jesus' mercy
is so powerful that it could transform into feelings of love Elder
Richards's very natural negative feelings about this wicked, cruel
man who did so much evil.

## The Abundance of Jesus' Love

This brings us to the second more excellent way. In addition to
boundless mercy, Jesus also shows us abundant love. We've refreshed
our minds about many of the miracles of healing he performed. Do
not our hearts swell with gratitude for the boundless mercy of the
Savior?

Now, think of the generosity of these miracles. It doesn't seem to
have mattered whether people begged miracles for themselves or for
their loved ones. Jesus willingly healed them all. It didn't matter
whether the sufferers were near at hand or far away. Jesus' power
extended as far as his perception of their need. A lot of people tried
to hush those who were calling out to Jesus. They thought these
people were being intrusive, indecorous, even rude. But Jesus didn't.
He saw their faith and was pleased.

Now, think of the abundant generosity of Jesus' miracles.

Remember the day that Jesus called Peter to become his disciple. To a tired, hungry fisherman who had fished all night without catching anything, Jesus performed a miracle that called so many fish to Peter that the nets started to break. And even with the help of his partner, there were so many fish that both boats were filled and began to sink. Think of the miracle of changing the water into wine at the wedding in Cana. He not only turned water into wine, but he made it the best wine that anyone had ever tasted. These are extravagant, lavish, generous miracles.

I don't believe that this abundance and generosity are accidental. Jesus told his followers: "Give, and it shall be given unto you; good measure, pressed down, and shaken together, and running over." And the context in which he spoke these words was one in which he asked us to be merciful. "Judge not, and ye shall not be judged," he said. "Condemn not, and ye shall not be condemned: forgive, and ye shall be forgiven" (Luke 6:37–38). This is an idea we will come back to.

President Howard W. Hunter gave us another concept to think about in his discussion of the miracle at the wedding at Cana:

> The first miracle by Jesus recorded in the New Testament was the turning of water into wine at the marriage at Cana. . . . But poor, indeed, was the making of the wine in the pots of stone, compared with its original making in the beauty of the vine and the abundance of the swelling grapes. No one could explain the onetime miracle at the wedding feast, but then neither could they explain the everyday miracle of the splendor of the vineyard itself.
>
> It is most remarkable to witness one who is deaf made to hear again, but surely that great blessing is no more startling than the wondrous combination of bones and skin and nerves that let our ears receive the beautiful world of sound. Should we not stand in awe of the blessing of hearing and

give glory to God for that miracle, even as we do when hearing is restored after it has been lost?

Is it not the same for the return of one's sight or the utterance of our speech, or even that greatest miracle of all—the restoration of life? The original creations of the Father constitute a truly wonder-filled world. Are not the *greatest* miracles the fact that we have life and limb and sight and speech in the first place? Yes, there will always be plenty of miracles if we have eyes to see and ears to hear.[6]

Do we have such eyes? Are we able to see the world we live in as one of miracles that reflects the abundant love and generosity of the Savior? Can we feel the outpouring of his mercy upon us? Can we have eyes to see and ears to hear that we are never alone or abandoned? Is this not a more excellent way than ingratitude, harshness, and pharisaism in keeping the rules?

## Withholding Judgment

Once we have received and savored the gifts offered to us by the Lord, we then realize that we can also offer gifts to each other. I want to concentrate on just two out of many gifts we might bestow: first, the gift of withholding judgment, and second, the gift of offering compassionate service.

In his Sermon on the Mount, Jesus said: "Judge not, that ye be not judged." This may sound like a warning or a restriction, but instead it is a glorious and exciting promise, because Jesus continues: "For with what judgment ye judge, ye shall be judged: and with what measure ye mete, it shall be measured to you again" (Matthew 7:1–2). What do we know about the measure of Christ? We have already pointed it out. It is an abundant measure, filled up, shaken together, pressed down, and running over. What is Jesus promising us here? If we are generous, tolerant, accepting, and loving, that's exactly how we will be treated.

Are any of us so righteous, so perfect in keeping all of the rules, so flawless and so sinless that we do not need this promise? Would you be so confident as to assemble your checklist of righteousness, march up to the Savior on the Day of Judgment, and declare, "I want exactly what's coming to me. I've earned every speck of celestial glory. Just look at this record!" I don't think so! I think all of us are going to be profoundly grateful for the mercy of God and for the abundant generosity of his measure.

Let's look again at Jesus' command not to judge others. He has something very specific in mind—fault-finding—for he continues:

> And why beholdest thou the mote that is in thy brother's eye, but considerest not the beam that is in thine own eye?
>
> Or how wilt thou say to thy brother, Let me pull out the mote out of thine eye; and, behold, a beam is in thine own eye?
>
> Thou hypocrite, first cast out the beam out of thine own eye; and then shalt thou see clearly to cast out the mote out of thy brother's eye. (Matthew 7:3–5.)

Let me rephrase this in more modern terms that we might be able to relate to.

> And why are you so upset by your sister's problem, or inconsistency, or weakness, when you have successfully managed to ignore the fact that you have the same problem?
>
> How could you say to Sister Brown, "Well, if you were home with your children like you're supposed to be, they wouldn't have had that water fight and tracked mud into the family room?" How could you say that when you were—yes, in the house with your children—but you'd scolded them and sent them to their rooms. There's no mud on your floor, but your heart was not with your children and you had no compassion for their tears and their loneliness.
>
> You insincere and self-righteous pretender, first see if you

can develop compassion for your own children before you make Sister Brown feel worse than she already does about the mud on her floor. At least her children were having fun together, and she didn't make them feel like criminals for it. Maybe you think she doesn't have a right to complain about the mud? Maybe not. But if she wants tips on how to be better organized so she doesn't have to run last-minute errands and leave her children alone, do you think she'll ask *you* for advice?

I'm sure that we all have failings that we feel guilty about that we fill in the blank with whatever we feel worst about. And *all* of us try sometimes to make ourselves feel better by making comparisons, if only mentally, by saying, "Well, at least I don't do such-and-such like Sister So-and-So."

Well, my belief is that Jesus liberates us from that terrible, unhappy, unpleasant burden. We don't have to judge ourselves and we don't have to judge others. I think of an example as reported in the *Church News* some time ago, from a patient and lovely woman who had the strength not to judge when she herself was being judged. It is a story told by Connie Kent, of Keizer, Oregon. She was responding to the topic, "How to Overcome Difficulties with Neighbors." She wrote:

> I have four boys who are quite rambunctious. At one time, we had neighbors on the other side of the back fence who had no children, and they were harsh in their judgments of our children. I never let myself get into a battle of words. I was always pleasant no matter what she said to me. One day she was upset at one of my boys. She told me they were moving and added that they were glad. I was pleasant in return and apologized for the times my boys upset her. Because I responded to her with kindness, she started to calm down. I learned from the experience that we need to understand

that sometimes our neighbors don't understand the mind-set we might have.[7]

I don't know what celestial reward Connie Kent will receive, but I think of the many rewards she experienced here on the earth: a peaceful heart instead of one filled with resentment and turmoil, enough love that she could love her rambunctious boys and her judgmental neighbor, and an empathy so broad that she could understand the point of view even of someone who was being unkind to her children. Think of all the burdens Connie Kent did *not* have to bear just because she refused to pick up the burden of judgment.

Jesus goes on to repeat the promise of generosity, just in case we didn't get it the first three or four times, as he continues in the Sermon on the Mount. He urges us:

> Ask, and it shall be given you; seek, and ye shall find; knock, and it shall be opened unto you:
>
> For every one that asketh receiveth; and he that seeketh findeth; and to him that knocketh it shall be opened.
>
> Or what man is there of you, whom if his son ask bread, will he give him a stone?
>
> Or if he ask for a fish, will he give him a serpent?
>
> If ye then, being evil, know how to give good gifts unto your children, how much more shall your Father which is in heaven give good things to them that ask him?

Then here's the verse we've all memorized as the golden rule:

> Therefore all things whatsoever ye would that men should do to you, do ye even so to them: for this is the law and the prophets. (Matthew 7:7–12.)

Wait a minute! Is Jesus saying that the Golden Rule is the law and the prophets? Is that really true? Can that possibly be what he meant? You mean that the law and the prophets doesn't mean going to meetings and doing genealogy and always bringing your scriptures to meetings and getting 100 percent visiting teaching? You mean that the law and the prophets doesn't mean attending the temple and giving out copies of the Book of Mormon and paying your tithing and keeping the Word of Wisdom? Well, of course all of these things are important, but what Jesus says is the most important is treating other people the way we'd like to be treated.

Really? That's it? Well, maybe so. Maybe we really can believe that simple kindness is what the gospel is all about. Because this wasn't the first time Jesus said something like this. Do you remember the occasion when a lawyer wanted to know what he had to do to inherit eternal life? Well, a lawyer knows about rules. He knows about what happens if you break rules. He makes his living, in fact, from advising and helping—or attacking—people who haven't been successful at keeping all the rules. Jesus responded with a question of his own. He asked: "What is written in the law? how readest thou?" In other words, he was saying, "You know the law. How do you interpret what it says? What are the most crucial, essential, and irreplaceable things that must be done to qualify for eternal life?"

The lawyer knew the answer. He was competent at his job, and he knew that there were two things that had to be done. He told Jesus: "Thou shalt love the Lord thy God with all thy heart, and with all thy soul, and with all thy strength, and with all thy mind; and thy neighbour as thyself." And Jesus agreed that these were, in fact, the two most important things (see Luke 10:25–27).

Isn't that wonderful? Loving our Heavenly Father and loving each other are essential if we are to gain eternal life. I don't know about you; but when I was teaching school, I quickly learned that if I had more than about five rules in the classroom, the children couldn't remember them. They got confused. And pretty soon, the rules started contradicting each other. So I had a very simple list of rules: (1) Take turns in everything, (2) Listen to instructions, (3) Listen to each other, and (4) Respect each other's rights. So you can see why I love the simplicity of the Lord's rules.

## Compassionate Service

The second of the two gifts we are to bestow is that of giving compassionate service to others. We can frequently identify the beginning point of abundant love, but we can never identify the ending point because we literally do not know where the influence of a thoughtful act will end.

The Apostle Paul, interestingly enough, uses the same phrase that appears in Ether. He tells the Corinthian Saints to "covet earnestly the best gifts"—meaning gifts of the Spirit, then continues: "and yet shew I unto you a more excellent way" (1 Corinthians 12:31). This is the verse immediately preceding that beautiful chapter on charity in 1 Corinthians 13 that begins: "Though I speak with the tongues of men and of angels, and have not charity, I am become as sounding brass, or a tinkling cymbal." This chapter is where the Relief Society motto, "Charity never faileth," comes from. So the point he is making is that the more excellent way is the way of love.

I want to share a story that will illustrate this point. It's from a woman of another faith, but the experience could almost be that of a visiting teacher.

She writes:

> The minister approached me after church. "We're going to check in with people who haven't been here for a while to make sure they're okay and let them know they're missed. Will you help?"
>
> It was the tenth anniversary of my mother's death, and visiting strangers was the last thing I wanted to do. "Not today," I said. "I'm sorry." As I left the church, I prayed, *Lord, I'd give anything to feel Mama near again.*
>
> For years after Mama died, I had met with her friends to laugh and talk, remembering her cheerful ways, her parties and how she made time to visit the housebound. The word

"visit" stung my conscience. I went back to the minister. "I'll help after all," I said, and he handed me a name and address.

When I drove to the house, a woman answered the door.

"I'm here to see Cora Heinecke," I said, introducing myself.

"Cora's in bed," the woman replied. "She's one hundred years old, you know. But she loves company."

She led me to a dark bedroom, where she raised the shades and told Cora, "You have a visitor. Mrs. Potter is from the church."

Cora sat up. "Lillian Layton's daughter?" she asked. "What a blessing!"

I looked at her, unbelieving. It turned out that Cora had been a close friend of my mother's! For more than an hour we talked about Mama.

It was a discovery I never have forgotten: When I reached out to others, Mama came nearer to me.[8]

Clearly, we do not know what blessings the Lord has prepared for those who are willing to walk in his way, to take those steps that he says are the more excellent way.

President Howard W. Hunter, speaking at general conference, gave all of us a powerful challenge when he said: "We must think more of holy things. . . . We should at every opportunity ask ourselves, 'What would Jesus do?' and then act more courageously upon the answer. We must be about his work as he was about his Father's. We should make every effort to become like Christ, the one perfect and sinless example this world has ever seen."[9] I was greatly struck by his saying that we need to act "courageously" upon the promptings we receive from the Spirit about living a Christlike life. I think there are times when doing the right thing can be frightening.

I subscribe to the *Pacific Citizen,* a publication of the Japanese American Citizen's League. I was very interested in a recent article about Yukiko Sugihara, the widow of Chiune Sugihara, who was a Japanese Schindler in his efforts to save the lives of Jews. He was serving as Japanese consul to Lithuania in 1939. Three times, he tried to obtain approval from the Japanese government to issue visas to Polish Jews so they could escape the Nazi atrocities and extermination orders. It is not clear whether he was refused or whether he simply did not get an answer, but finally, without approval and, consequently, at great risk to himself and his family, he decided to issue the transit visas. Before he was sent back to Japan, he wrote some 2,000 visas and arranged fictitious marriages so that the maximum number of people could be carried on each document. He helped 6,000 Jews escape. I have heard stories that he wrote the last of these visas and pushed them out the window of his compartment as the train was pulling away from the station. Mrs. Sugihara said that her husband had been converted to Christianity while he was living in Harbin, Manchuria. As a Christian, he felt compelled to act with compassion. As a samurai, he felt compelled to make his own honorable decisions. His dual allegiance was a life-giving combination.

Mrs. Sugihara was honored at a program in Sacramento where other Holocaust survivors also spoke. Rabbi Samuel Gradenz, then living in Modesto, had been in Lithuania and had helped Sugihara pass out the visas and arrange the marriages. He still carries in his pocket his own much-tattered visa—his passport to life.

Someone else participating in the tribute was Shira Takeshita of San Leandro, California. As a young man, he was sent to the relocation center in Poston, Arizona. He enlisted in the 522nd Field Artillery Battalion. He told how, fifty years ago, he was part of the American force that liberated Dachau. What he thought were "piles of snow" turned out to be the bodies of dead Jews piled up in heaps, "the sight and stench of which I could never forget."

Solly Ganor came from Israel to also speak on the program. As an eleven-year-old boy, he was one of the survivors liberated at

Dachau by the Nisei soldiers of the 522nd Field Artillery. He remembers his surprise at seeing soldiers in American uniforms but with "oriental faces." Some thought that Japan had won the war.[10]

In this case, it is easy to see why doing the right thing took courage. Mrs. Sugihara did not describe her own feelings during this extraordinary ordeal, but surely she and her children also shared the danger that her husband courageously took upon himself. Surely they were also placed at risk by his Christian compassion.

I think the fear that we must confront and deal with is just as real, even though it may not endanger our lives. How much courage does it take, when gossiping is going on, to say, "I can't imagine saying things like this if Sister So-and-So were here, so I don't feel comfortable talking about her in her absence." How much courage does it take, when you see that someone is being excluded, even unintentionally, to reach out and draw her into your circle? How much courage does it take in a Relief Society class to raise your hand when everyone seems to agree on only one point of view but where it seems to contradict the Savior's law of love?

When Ed and I first came to Utah in the early 1950s, it was not long after World War II, and many people had hard feelings against Japanese people because of the war. We heard many things that hurt us and made us realize that people felt we were different, even in the Church. I was teaching grade school, and one day my principal, Edith Ryberg, told me with great sadness and some shock about an experience she had had the previous day in Sunday School.

"You'll never believe it," she said. "The teacher said that people who weren't born in the covenant hadn't been as valiant in the preexistence as the rest of us and that they wouldn't reach the highest degree of the celestial kingdom. I couldn't stand it. I stood up, told them about you, and asked, 'Do you mean to tell me that Chieko Okazaki, who converted herself at age fifteen, is not going to be in the highest degree of the celestial kingdom if she keeps on being righteous?' The teacher just nodded. I argued and argued, Chieko," Edith said, "but the whole class agreed with him."

That was a painful experience for me. It was a painful experience for my friend and principal. But knowing that she had the courage to speak the truth of the gospel for me was a bright and shining light to me in a wilderness of intolerance and racial prejudice that could have seemed very dark. I had heard things like that myself, and no Edith was there to say, "Just a minute. That's not the way *I* understand the gospel."

Many things have changed since then. In the past fifty years, those people who agreed that no convert could receive complete exaltation sent their children and grandchildren and great-grandchildren on missions all over the world. They came to see the ugliness of what had been done to a racial minority in Germany and to the interned Japanese in their own country. They came to understand the gospel differently, more fully, more beautifully. It is unthinkable that such a thing would be said in any Sunday School class today.

I forgave it long ago, and I know that Heavenly Father has forgiven it too. But I have never forgotten it because there are many other people who sit in our meetings and shrink inside, suffering invisible wounds inflicted by thoughtless people who interpret the gospel in ways that exclude. I have listened with many ears other than my own to lessons in Relief Society or Sunday School. I have listened with the ears of a battered wife to statements asserting that it is the woman's responsibility to follow her husband, and I have raised my hand to comment that this is true, but at the same time, it is *his* responsibility to lead in a righteous direction.

I have listened with the ears of the childless woman when a lesson has talked exclusively about how to teach a gospel principle to children, and I have raised my hand to ask, "How might this principle benefit someone who has no children?"

I have listened with the ears of a divorced man or woman when a teacher has talked about how divorce is caused by selfishness. I have raised my hand to separate the sins that may lead to divorce from the fact of divorce itself and to praise the many single parents I know who are mature, compassionate, and effective.

In nearly every case, the teacher has had no intention of being hurtful to the person sitting there quietly. He or she simply had not seen the individual they had thoughtlessly condemned or offended.

Well, Jesus did not overlook people. He looked into eyes and into hearts. He valued, taught, and healed each person who came to him. This is a joyful talent I think we were all born with, no matter how shy we may feel or lacking in courage. If we ask ourselves, "What would the Savior do in this circumstance?" I think the answer will come quickly. Knowing is easy, but doing is harder.

In any church meeting we attend, if it matches the statistical profile, there are at least some among us who are survivors of childhood sexual abuse or rape or crimes of personal violence, often committed by members of their own family. In that room are those who are surviving the ongoing pain of divorce, of wasted potential, of faltering faith, of bearing the wounds of a beloved child or sibling who has used his or her free agency to make terrible choices that have brought great suffering to himself or herself and others. In your family, or in the family of someone close to you, someone is working through the difficult realizations of homosexuality, of chronic physical illness, of mental or emotional instability, of chemical dependency, of injustice, of sorrow, of loneliness, of discouragement. Some of you already know the enormous strength that comes from sharing this burden with someone else who cares for you. Some of you are trying to carry these burdens alone or are struggling with the even heavier burden of denial and pretense.

Please, don't try to do it alone, and don't make a brother or a sister do it alone. Recognize that no one can carry our burdens for us, except the Savior. Recognize that we are here in mortality as a free choice to have experiences with both joy and sorrow. There is, of course, a line of appropriateness between sharing your sorrow and broadcasting complaints. I ask you to be sensitive to the struggles of your fellow Church members—to offer a hand to lift a burden where you can, to be a listening ear when speaking will ease an over-burdened heart, to seek out a compassionate friend who will under-stand and reassure and strengthen you at times that are difficult for you.

For me, knowing the Savior's love and feeling it within me makes it joyful to reach out to others with that same love. I think that this is what it means to bear one another's burdens. Let me share with you a beautiful poem about the spirit of consecration, written over a hundred years ago.

> Take my life and let it be
> Consecrated, Lord, to thee;
> Take my moments and my days,
> Let them flow in ceaseless praise.
> Take my hands and let them move
> At the impulse of thy love;
> Take my feet and let them be
> Swift and beautiful for thee.
> Take my voice and let me sing
> Always, only, for my King;
> Take my lips and let them be
> Filled with messages from Thee.
> Take my silver and my gold,
> Not a mite would I withhold;
> Take my intellect and use
> Every power as Thou shalt choose.
> Take my love, my Lord, I pour
> At Thy feet its treasured store;
> Take myself, and I will be
> Ever, only, all, for Thee.[11]

Think of the great joy we can bring into a troubled world by consecrating ourselves to selfless acts of compassion and love.

## Conclusion

To review where we have been, think about words of wisdom, about candles and birthday cakes, about false teeth, and about picking up speed. I hope in the thoughts we've shared together, you've also had some concepts and insights come to you. We have rejoiced in our testimonies of the endless mercy and the abundant love of Jesus Christ, and we've contemplated our ability to offer two gifts to others in return: the gift of withholding judgment and the gift of compassionate service.

Please remember that Jesus measures out his mercies to us as abundantly as his love. Remember the remarkable dream that came to Apostle George F. Richards in the aftermath of a war that was caused by a man whose evilness no one can doubt. Remember that we are not limited to our own resources in loving or we would run out fast, but we have a universe of love to draw on.

Think of Mrs. Potter and the gift of an hour's memories of her mother from a woman she hadn't wanted to visit. Walk the more excellent way in faith that, truly, Christ is "the way."

Let me conclude with one more story to encourage us when we try to be kind and loving and patient and merciful by drawing only on our own limited resources. Suzanne was a tall teenager, which everyone thought would make her a great basketball player, but she was so awkward that she was sure her P. E. grades were going to keep her out of college. At the beginning of her junior year in high school, the basketball coach asked if anyone would be willing to forego basketball to teach Henry how to swim. Henry was a freshman with some mental handicaps. Suzanne volunteered immediately, thinking it would be a cinch. This is what happened:

> Tuesday, I met Henry. This is going to be easy, I thought.
> . . . I'll just sit on the side and tell Henry what to do.

Wednesday I was in the water with Henry.

Thursday I was ready to drown Henry.

By Friday, basketball was looking good.

At first he just thought it was a game, and he wouldn't even try. I got so frustrated. . . . Weeks had gone by. He was still messing around, and I was still yelling.

. . . "Make him teachable," I prayed. "Please help him to listen to me and cooperate."

Henry was no different the next day or the next. However, when I saw Henry, I noticed what a sweet smile he had. Then I laughed at something silly he did. I stopped yelling. . . . I sat on the edge of the pool with him and told him how dangerous it was not to know how to swim. I told him he had to learn how because I wanted him to be safe. I told him, "I care what happens to you," and I meant it.

Henry started trying. He put his face in the water. He kicked. He practiced his arms. He floated when I held him. . . . By the last day, he made it across the short end of the pool. . . . I've never seen anyone look so proud.

. . . I did such a small thing for Henry, and yet I reaped great benefits. His learning how to swim even got me an A in P.E. that semester. And I learned a very important lesson from Henry. I thought Heavenly Father had ignored my prayer because Henry didn't change. Yet *he* didn't have to. *I* was the person who needed a softened heart, and I got it. . . .

I also learned that Heavenly Father cares about each of us. And he wants us to care about each other.[12]

I testify that we are infinitely precious to the Lord. He loves us. His mercy is endless. Our Lord and Savior has taught us how to be merciful. He came to earth to show us the way and to be the way. He did not hesitate even at the point of death for us. And his compassion is our only hope of righteousness in this world and salvation in the world to come.

As members of the Church, we are the household of faith. We stand as watchpersons upon the walls of Zion. We hold up the light of Christ. Our hands are swift with the healing balm of mercy and charity. We have received richly and freely from the Savior. Generously and freely, we must give. Let each of our associations with each other be gifts of mercy, abundance, acceptance, and compassion to each other.

# 7

# By Their Fruits:
# Mary, Martha, and Lazarus

*W*hen you consider Jesus' comment, "By their fruits ye shall know them" (Matthew 7:20), do you ever ask yourself, "What are the fruits of my life?" I do. I ask what fruits I want to bring forth. What fruits do I want to be known for? I have pondered these questions many times over my lifetime, and the answers are nearly always the same. First, I want the peace of mind that comes from knowing the Savior. Second, I want to serve; I want to make a positive difference in the lives of other people.

While considering these two fruits that I desire in my own life, I was reminded of the story in the New Testament of the two sisters, Mary and Martha. And then I remembered their brother Lazarus, whom Christ raised from the dead, and I realized that I also want to add a third fruit: I want to become one who loves and responds to the voice of Jesus Christ so that he can call me forth into new life even from the bondage of spiritual death.

## Choosing the Better Part

There are three stories about this family in the New Testament, so let's begin by reviewing what we know about them. For one thing, Martha was apparently the oldest, even though we usually reverse the order of the names and say "Mary and Martha." But John, who tells all three of the stories, says that it was Martha's house that Jesus visited. They lived in Bethany, which is a little less than two miles from Jerusalem. We don't know how they first met Jesus nor why they responded to him so strongly nor why he gave them such a special place in his heart, but John informs us, "Jesus loved Martha, and her sister, and Lazarus," and when the sisters sent word that Lazarus was dangerously ill, they described their brother by saying, "Lord, behold, he whom thou lovest is sick" (John 11:5, 3).

There is no mention made of husbands for the sisters nor a wife for Lazarus and no mention of parents either. According to Matthew, the third story about Mary and Martha takes place in the house of Simon the Leper (see Matthew 26:6). Since no leper would have been allowed to entertain guests, Simon must have been healed of his leprosy; and in that case, he had almost certainly been healed by Jesus since no cure was known in biblical times. Yet since that house is identified as Martha's and since Martha has twice served the meal, the relationship of these individuals is not clear. Jeni and Richard Holzapfel point out that it was "socially inappropriate" in Jesus' day for a man "to enter a home or be served by a woman who was not his wife or relative. Women did not normally eat with men whenever there was a guest present, nor did the women normally serve the men if a boy or slave were available."[1] It appears then that Martha, Mary, and Lazarus were three siblings sharing a household, in which their father was ill. In any case, their situation was unusual for the times but a good reminder to us that Jesus loves all kinds of families, not just those that are fortunate enough to have a father, a mother, and children.

We know very little about Lazarus. In all three of these stories, he never says a word. He is completely silent. Perhaps he was younger than the two sisters, but he was not a child because the scriptures say "a certain *man* was sick, named Lazarus" (John 11:1; emphasis added).

And like other families, there is a certain amount of squabbling and disharmony going on when we first meet them.

According to Luke, Martha "received him into her house" and

Mary "sat at Jesus' feet, and heard his word." You remember what happened next. Martha was upset over all the work she had to do; so she came to Jesus and said, "Lord, dost thou not care that my sister hath left me to serve alone? bid her therefore that she help me." Jesus answered her, "Martha, Martha, thou art careful and troubled about many things: But one thing is needful; and Mary hath chosen that good part, which shall not be taken away from her" (Luke 10:38–42).

One aspect of this story has always been very troubling to me. It's the implication that Martha is wrong to be concerned about the work or, as the King James Version puts it, "cumbered about much serving." That's always seemed unfair to me. I know how much work it takes to prepare food for a large party, and Jesus, of course, was accompanied by his disciples. That's thirteen hungry men to feed, and you don't do that by snapping your fingers.

And Lazarus! We don't even know where he is during this story. If he's present, he's there in the background; but is he in the kitchen helping Martha or is he in the courtyard listening to Jesus talking to Mary? And if he's not there, then where is he? We don't know.

Why did Luke include it? He doesn't usually spend a whole lot of time writing on hospitality and entertainment, so I think he thought the point of the story was in Jesus' statement to Martha that "one thing is needful: and Mary hath chosen that good part, which shall not be taken away from her" (Luke 10:42). What is the "one needful thing"—the one thing that is essential, indispensable, that Mary can't do without? I believe it's to choose Jesus—to be his disciple, to learn from him. I can accept that. I can see how it could be more important than feeding thirteen hungry men.

There are other things to consider about this story. Jesus doesn't tell Martha that she's wrong. He doesn't tell her to stop picking on Mary. We know that he cares about the physical welfare of people who listen to him, or he wouldn't have fed the five thousand. He doesn't pretend that food isn't important. He also uses an odd phrase: Mary's "good part . . . shall not be taken away from her." The message would be very different if he said, "Mary's chosen the good part and I'm not going to take it away from her and neither are you." That would have made it a very adversarial situation. Instead, he seems to be simply describing the results of Mary's choice. Because she has exercised her agency in making this righteous choice, Martha *cannot* and Jesus *will* not take her discipleship away from her.

In other words, if it's humanly possible to tell Mary that she's right without also telling Martha that she's wrong, then Jesus does it. But it's possible that he's also inviting Martha to make the same choice. Did you notice that he says, "Martha, Martha!" There are some other places in the scriptures where someone is called twice by name. For instance, when God established his covenant with Jacob, he called him, "Jacob, Jacob." When he woke the boy Samuel from sleep, calling him to his future work as a prophet, he said, "Samuel! Samuel!" And when the Lord spoke to Saul on the road to Damascus, he again called him twice, "Saul, Saul."[2]

So perhaps instead of chastising Martha, Jesus was really inviting her to also accept the call of discipleship.

The problem is, we don't know because the story ends there. Did Martha put down her basket and cease setting the table and let the fire go out under the lentils while she and Mary both sat at the feet of Jesus? Maybe. But if she did, then what about the thirteen hungry men? There are possibilities, but we just don't know. Whatever took place did so behind a closed curtain.

I know I'm not the only woman who is troubled by the contradictions in this story. Let me share with you two poems on the dichotomy between Mary and Martha. The first is by a friend of mine from Colorado, Launie Severinsen:

> My hands are those of Martha,
> With much serving cumbered about.
> Home duties continue to keep me

> So busy my time just runs out.
> Oh, no, I don't belittle
> These tasks, that's very true.
> For I know motherhood's important
> As is each thing I must do.
> Still I long to know of the Master,
> To study the words He spake,
> That I might grow in wisdom,
> And correct decisions make.
> But consumed by physical troubles,
> As pressures abound and build,
> My spirit self becomes empty,
> Though my every moment is filled.
> At these times, I desire as Mary,
> To choose "that good part,"
> Though my hands are the hands of Martha,
> I am Mary in my heart.[3]

I think this is a good way to resolve the dilemma, at least temporarily. Our bodies can be Martha and our hearts can be Mary. We can pursue our duties as mothers and workers as efficiently and effectively as Martha while keeping a place in our hearts for meditating on the Savior and his words of life.

I don't know the author of this second poem, but I can tell that it was also written by a woman. She writes:

> Lord of all pots and pans and things.
> Since I've no time to be
> A saint by doing lovely things,
> Or watching late with Thee,
> Or dreaming in the dawnlight,
> Or storming heaven's gates,
> Make me a saint by getting meals,
> And washing up the plates.

Although I have Martha's hands,
I have a Mary's mind;
And when I black the boots and shoes,
Thy sandals, Lord, I find.
I think of how they trod the earth,
Each time I scrub the floor.
Accept this meditation, Lord,
I haven't time for more.
Warm all the kitchen with Thy love,
And light it with Thy peace;
Forgive me all my worrying,
And make all grumbling cease.
Thou who didst love to give men food,
In a room or by the sea,
Accept this service that I do—
I do it unto Thee.[4]

I think that this is also a good way to solve the dilemma. We can consecrate the necessary tasks that we do as acts of worship and service, knowing that Jesus will accept our service to others as service done to him.

It helps me to approach this difficult story by asking, What were the fruits for Mary? What were the fruits for Martha? In both cases, the fruits were good. This may be one of those choices that we must sometimes make—not between good and evil but between two good things.

## The Raising of Lazarus

The second story involves the raising of Lazarus from the dead, and this story convinces me that we are missing some important details that Luke didn't provide. It helps us fill in a few of those blanks. This story, which takes all of John 11, is where we learn that Jesus loved all three of them, "Martha, and her sister, and Lazarus." I think it may be important that Martha's name comes first. To me, it says that Jesus didn't view Martha as just too materialistic and non-spiritual to have a testimony of him. It doesn't say that he loved Mary and Lazarus and merely tolerated Martha because she was a good cook. No, it says that he *loved* all three of them.

And I think Martha must have accepted the Savior's invitation to become his disciple because when he takes his disciples and goes to Bethany after the death of Lazarus, she is the one who goes to meet him while Mary remains in the house. This is pure speculation on my part, but if my beloved only brother was dying and I knew Jesus could save him and Jesus delayed his coming for two days, I'd want to know the reason why. Maybe Mary couldn't face Jesus with that question. Maybe she felt betrayed and abandoned or was sunk so deeply in her grief that she did not even have hope. She could not be separated from Jesus' presence in the first story, but now, for whatever reason, she doesn't go to seek him.

Martha does go out to meet him, and the first words she speaks are "Lord, if thou hadst been here, my brother had not died. But I know, that even now, whatsoever thou wilt ask of God, God will give it thee" (John 11:21–22). What tone of voice did she use? Was she angry? Was she pleading? Was she grief stricken? It sounds to me as if she had reduced the paradox to its simplest and starkest dimensions. Martha was no fool. She knew that dead was dead. But she also knew that Jesus was the master of life and death and that God would grant Jesus any request.

Often we have to face irreconcilable paradoxes. We have a patriarchal blessing that promises us a husband and children, yet the years go by and we remain unmarried. We faithfully hold family home evening every week, and our teenager ends up in juvenile detention for shoplifting. Our mother, who has served others generously and compassionately all of her life, has Alzheimer's and can't even recognize us any more. How do we reconcile the promises, the way things are supposed to be, with the way things are? This was Martha's dilemma.

Jesus resolves the paradox for her in this next thrilling passage.

Jesus saith unto her, Thy brother shall rise again.

Martha saith unto him, I know that he shall rise again in the resurrection at the last day.

Jesus said unto her, I am the resurrection, and the life: he that believeth in me, though he were dead, yet shall he live:

And whosoever liveth and believeth in me shall never die. (vv. 23–26.)

Then he asks Martha the question that every paradox asks: "Believest thou this?" And Martha answers with the testimony of a true disciple. In an expression that echoes that of Peter, she says: "Yea, Lord: I believe that thou art the Christ, the Son of God, which should come into the world" (v. 26–27).

Now, if there is any question at all in anybody's mind about what happened in the kitchen while Martha was serving and Mary was sitting at Jesus' feet, if there is any concern that a Martha cannot be spiritual, or that someone who is organizing food for thirteen hungry men is too preoccupied with trifles to understand the important things of life, remember Martha's testimony. She recognized Jesus as the Son of God. Even in this hour of grief and bewilderment and pain, she heard his voice and knew who he really was.

Martha then "secretly" tells Mary that Jesus is waiting to speak to her, and Mary hastens to him, falls at his feet weeping, and says the exact same words that Martha used, "Lord, if thou hadst been here, my brother had not died" (v. 32). But she doesn't have an implied question as Martha does. The absence of Jesus means the absence of her brother, and her grief overcomes her.

I think it's important to recognize that Jesus responded to each of the sisters according to her individual need. Martha needed an answer. And she got an answer. Mary needed sympathy, a recognition of her pain. And that's what she got:

When Jesus therefore saw her weeping, and the Jews also weeping which came with her, he groaned in the spirit, and was troubled,

And said, Where have ye laid him? They said unto him, Lord, come and see.

Jesus wept.

Then said the Jews, Behold how he loved him! (vv. 33–36.)

Jesus came to the tomb, "again groaning in himself" (v. 38.) He felt Mary's pain. He shared Mary's pain. He mourned with this mourning sister. My friend Launie shared with me an amazing insight into this scripture. "That [Jesus] was troubled seeing their sorrow, that he paused to weep with them as they wept, seems to me the very best example of charity, for he knew that in a very few moments he would return their brother to them alive, yet he had compassion for them in their time of sorrow."[5]

The feeling would have been so different if he had said, "Mary, everything's really all right. Stop crying. I'm going to raise Lazarus from the dead. You don't have to feel bad." Instead, he shared her suffering; and from the foundation of that compassion, he reached out to restore Lazarus.

## The Supper at Bethany

In the third story involving Martha, Mary, and Lazarus, which is recorded in Mark, Matthew, and John, the setting could almost be a repetition of the first story. "They made him a supper," the scripture reads, "and Martha served." But this time, she isn't described as "cumbered with the much serving" and she doesn't complain that Mary isn't helping her. Lazarus is present now, too, as "one of them that sat at the table with [Jesus]" (John 12:2). According to the Greek text, Jesus and Lazarus and the other men "followed Greco-Roman custom and 'reclined' or laid on a mat while leaning on the left arm, thereby keeping the right hand free for eating the food placed on a low table."[6]

Once again, Mary is at Jesus' feet, but instead of just listening to his teachings, she took "a pound of ointment of spikenard, very costly, and anointed the feet of Jesus, and wiped his feet with her hair: and the house was filled with the odour of the ointment" (v. 3). Mark and Matthew also recount this story, although John is the only Gospel writer to give her a name. All of them agree that she performed this act in worship, love, and reverence, that someone present protested at the extravagance, and that Jesus defended her action, saying, "Let her alone: against the day of my burying hath she kept this" (John 12:7).

The three sources all agree on the costliness of the ointment she used. Spikenard "is a fragrant oil derived from the root and spike . . . of the nard plant, which grows in the mountains of northern India." Its "sweet smell . . . filled the house."[7] Judas complains that she had spent 300 pence on it, an extravagant amount of money, which Judas suggested might well have been given to the poor. Yet Jesus, a homeless man who owned nothing except the clothes he wore, did not share Judas's concern. He perhaps saw that his apostle was not acting out of compassion for the poor but out of greed, and that this woman was acting in recognition of his coming burial.

This defense is notable because Peter, the apostle who had a testimony of Jesus' identity by direct revelation, had just showed his lack of complete understanding of Jesus' mission by rebuking Jesus when he said he would be slain and rise again (see Mark 8:31–32). Presumably the other apostles had also refused to believe that Jesus was on his way to his last Passover.

The scriptural record nowhere says that Jesus had shared the same teachings with Mary, Martha, and Lazarus; but I believe that he had done so and that Mary had combined two ceremonial acts. First, in cleansing his feet, she was performing the duty of a host to wash the dusty feet of his guests before a banquet. By wiping his feet with her hair, she was showing him the utmost respect, since she was using her own hair instead of a towel. Second, in anointing his feet, she was foreseeing and honoring his coming death. It was the custom of the time to anoint the head of a living guest who was being honored, but not the feet. It *was*, however, the custom to anoint the feet of a deceased person with scented oils.[8]

As Mark and Matthew report the incident, she anointed his head, suggesting that she anointed both his head and his feet—his head as her guest but also as the kings of ancient Israel were anointed by the prophets. If this is what happened, then Mary was acting prophetically in identifying Jesus as the Messiah, or the "anointed one." The Greek name "Christ" is Greek for "anointed."[9] Thus, Mary became a witness of the Savior's divinity.

I can't even begin to imagine what this gesture might have meant to Jesus as he prepared himself mentally and spiritually for his coming entrance into Jerusalem, his arrest, the Atonement, and his crucifixion. He knew that his apostles had not fully understood his mission and that one of them would even betray him. He knew that he had very little time to complete his important teachings. He had been misunderstood so many times, but this woman, this disciple, understood his mission, accepted the need for his atoning sacrifice, and worshipped him as her Lord and Savior as well as loving him as her friend and teacher.

Let's ask again: what were the fruits of Martha? What were the fruits of Mary? I believe we can see at this point that they were exactly the same. Both sisters were devoted and loving disciples of Jesus Christ. They understood who he was. They accepted his redeeming mission on their behalf. They expressed faith in him. They served him, each in her own way, and Jesus accepted equally the service of each.

And finally, in this story, I think I see the answer to that troubling first story. Martha accepts her sister's service to Jesus. She does not judge Mary's service or condemn her because it is different from her own. Jesus accepts Martha's discipleship and service as expressed in cooking and serving. He accepts Mary's discipleship as expressed in listening to him and anointing him. And finally, Martha accepts Mary's discipleship as equal to and just as valid as her own.

The problem in the first story wasn't that *Jesus* was judging one form of service as superior to the other. The problem was that *Martha* was making that judgment. And now, in this third story, we see that the sisters also understood each other, accepted each other, loved each other, did not judge each other, but blessed each other.

In this third story, neither Matthew, Mark, nor John records anything that Mary, Martha, or Lazarus says. In a way, that's appropriate. They had no need for speech because they had reached a perfect understanding. "Ye shall know them by their fruits. . . . A good tree cannot bring forth evil fruit, neither can a corrupt tree bring forth good fruit" (Matthew 7:16, 18). For both Mary and Martha, the fruit was their testimony of Jesus Christ. And they showed this good fruit in the ways that were best for each one of them—Mary in learning and in worship, Martha in service.

Is there a lesson for us? I think so. We all long to be disciples of the Lord Jesus Christ. We all long to worship him in holiness and beauty. We all long to serve those among us who are the least, because in so doing we serve Jesus himself. We all need to know that our worship is accepted and that our service is accepted. And perhaps most importantly, we need to know that Jesus himself accepts both the worship and the service. We do not need to judge another's service. We do not need to try to persuade or force anyone else to serve in our way. Jesus calls each one of us to discipleship and from each one of us he accepts our gestures of devotion and our acts of service.

For me, that is a very liberating message.

## Lazarus

What might we say about Lazarus, the silent brother? All of us have been ill and some of us have been seriously ill, perhaps enough that it has been life-threatening, but none of us have been that sick and been without medicine, without pain-relievers, or without antibiotics. We don't know why Lazarus was ill, but we can assume that it must have been painful. He must have known that he was on the point of death. He must have known that his sisters had sent for Jesus, and perhaps he even knew that Jesus had not come as he began slipping off into the final darkness. How did he reconcile his faith in Jesus with the fact of Jesus' absence? How did he reconcile the fact that he loved Jesus and knew Jesus loved him with the fact that Jesus had not come?

Then Lazarus died. In ancient Palestine, the body had to be buried almost immediately, usually before sundown if the person had died before noon but certainly within twenty-four hours. According to Jeni and Richard Holzapfel, the "customary preparation" of the body for burial was this:

> The eyes were closed, the entire body was washed and anointed with oil, and the hands and feet were then wrapped in linen bands. The body, clothed in a favorite garment, was then wrapped around with winding sheets. Spices of myrrh and aloes were placed in the folds of the garment to perfume the body. A napkin was then bound from the chin to the head, and the body was laid out for viewing.[10]

We assume that all of these customs were observed in the case of Lazarus's death, so that Mary and Martha washed him, anointed him, dressed and wrapped him, mourned for him, followed his body as it was borne to the sepulcher and laid away, and then stood by as the stone was rolled across the entrance. As chief mourners, they would be the focus of those who came to comfort them. It was part of the mourning ritual to fast and to keep a vigil, to dress in sackcloth and to put ashes on their heads. Perhaps Martha and Mary also followed this custom.

Meanwhile, what of Lazarus? His spirit was in paradise, where he would have learned, surely with great joy, that his faith in Jesus and his love for Jesus had not been misplaced, that Jesus was the Son of God, the Savior of the world. He would have understood the plan of salvation. It is reasonable to assume he would have also known that Jesus had been foreordained before the foundation of the world to die for the sins of mankind and that, in the calendar of crucial events, the pivotal event of the Atonement was very near. I wonder if Lazarus didn't also understand why Jesus had not come and that his (Lazarus's) death was to be a type and shadow of the Savior's own imminent death and subsequent resurrection.

Some of this is only speculation on my part because we do not have any information at all, but people who have out-of-body experiences and have been revived frequently report that they do not want to return to their bodies, that their spirits experience perfect joy, brightness, peace, and beauty and that their bodies seem a kind of imprisonment to them again. Perhaps it was so for Lazarus.

Even though Lazarus must have wanted to return to comfort his sisters and to see Jesus again in the flesh, I can imagine that it must have been an enormous sacrifice for him to return to his body and take up the business of living again. Because Heavenly Father honors and respects our agency so much, I'm sure that Lazarus gave willing consent, even if he may have preferred to remain in the spirit world. He had to know and he had to agree, even though he must also have understood that he would have to endure the grief of knowing that his friend and master, Jesus, was going to die and even though he himself would have to re-experience mortal death for the second time at some point in the future.

What happened in those moments of transition when Jesus prayed to Heavenly Father, then "cried with a loud voice, Lazarus, come forth"? (John 11:43). Did Lazarus feel his spirit reentering his body? Did he shrink from that task but carry through with it out of his great love for Jesus and his willingness to be obedient in all things? Did he feel his heart begin to beat again in response to the command of the Lord of life and death? What were his first thoughts when he realized that his spirit was once again residing in his body and that his body was encumbered about with burial clothes exactly as his spirit was now encumbered by his body?

The only thing we know is that he obeyed immediately: "And he that was dead came forth, bound hand and foot with graveclothes: and his face was bound about with a napkin. Jesus saith unto them, Loose him, and let him go" (v. 44). With what reverence and joyous haste the sisters, no longer sorrowing, freed Lazarus from his winding sheet! With what joy Lazarus must have embraced the Savior and looked into his eyes—Lazarus who had been called back from death's embrace, Jesus who would so soon pass into that embrace, if only temporarily.

I think I understand why Lazarus said nothing during the supper at Bethany while Martha served and Mary anointed Jesus' feet. What *could* he say? What did he remember? What did he understand? And even if he remembered perfectly everything that had transpired in the spirit world, how could he have described it? We simply don't know. He must have watched Mary anointing Jesus' feet and perhaps his head and realized that only a few days earlier, Mary had similarly anointed his own feet and hands and head as he lay dead.

I wonder what these three thought in Bethany when the news came that Jesus had been crucified. I wonder what they said as they sat together through the storm and the earthquake. Did they weep or had they already leaped ahead to the glorious fact of the resurrection? Surely Martha repeated over and over what Jesus had told her: "I am the resurrection, and the life: he that believeth in me, though he were dead, yet shall he live: And whosoever liveth and believeth in me shall never die" (vv. 25–26). They had already seen a great miracle. Did they lack faith to believe in the greatest miracle of all, the Resurrection, even before it happened? I don't think so.

From the point of view of the chief priests, nothing worse could have happened than this miracle. Because of Lazarus, indisputably raised from the dead in the presence of witnesses, after four days and when his mortal remains had already begun to decay, says John, "many of the Jews . . . believed on Jesus. . . . But the chief priests consulted that they might put Lazarus also to death" (John 12:10–11).

I don't know about you, but to me there is something pathetic and terrible about these chief priests turning away from the joy of this miracle to not only pursue their blood anger against Jesus but to expand their hatred also toward Lazarus, the recipient of the miracle.

I don't think Lazarus worried about their threats and plots too much. Another characteristic of people who return from near-death experiences is that death loses all terror for them. They see it for what it is, a doorway into a glorious new life, not terrifying, not threatening.

## Conclusion

What were the fruits by which we know Mary? They are the fruits of discipleship—the peace that passeth understanding that comes from knowing Jesus and knowing that he is the Savior—which she manifested in *worship.*

What were the fruits by which we know Martha? They are also the fruits of discipleship—the pure knowledge that "thou art the Christ, the Son of God, which should come into the world" (John 11:27)—which manifested itself in *service.*

What were the fruits by which we know Lazarus? We know him as one who heard the voice of his Lord even in the kingdom of the dead and responded without hesitation, his spirit reclothed in mortal flesh, encumbered with graveclothes, and coming forth from the prison of the tomb in similitude of the resurrection that Christ himself would achieve in only a few short days.

The three of them could say with the Apostle Paul: "But the fruit of the Spirit is love, joy, peace, longsuffering, gentleness, goodness, faith, meekness, [and] temperance" (Galatians 5:22–23). As the Apostle James said, "But the wisdom that is from above is first pure, then peaceable, gentle, and easy to be intreated, full of mercy and good fruits, without partiality, and without hypocrisy. And the fruit of righteousness is sown in peace of them that make peace" (James 3:17–18).

We can only imagine what holy thoughts and feelings Mary, Martha, and Lazarus experienced as they ministered to the Lord and received his blessings during mortality, but Jesus promises all of us the same intimate love. He considers us candidates to be the first fruits of the resurrection. By revelation to the Prophet Joseph Smith, the Savior has revealed that at his second coming:

> . . . The saints that are upon the earth, who are alive, shall be quickened and be caught up to meet him.
>
> And they who have slept in their graves shall come forth, for their graves shall be opened; and they also shall be caught up to meet him in the midst of the pillar of heaven—
>
> They are Christ's, the first fruits, they who shall descend with him first, and they who are on the earth and in their graves, who are first caught up to meet him; and all this by the voice of the sounding of the trump of the angel of God. (D&C 88:96–98.)

May we learn that Jesus accepts all discipleship, all worship, all service, and learn to free ourselves from the burden of judging and coercing others to serve our way or to worship after our fashion. May we hunger to sit at his feet and worship, as did Mary. May we yearn to serve him through the simple acts of carrying out our daily responsibilities as did Martha. May we attune our hearts so truly to his voice that we will hear it and respond, even to a whisper, as it reaches through the tomb of our spiritual death of sin and indifference and pride so that we, too, will arise and come forth into the sunlight of pure knowledge that he is our Savior and into the embrace of him who calls us to his eternal life. And may "the peace of God, which passeth all understanding, . . . keep [our] hearts and minds through Christ Jesus" (Philippians 4:7).

# 8

## Feeling Sisterly

*L*et's think about the power of feeling sisterly, one toward another. To start out, I'd like to pretend I'm having a private lunch with each one of you and that I've brought a Japanese lunchbox to make the experience more real. Such a lunchbox is beautifully designed. It consists of four lacquer bowls, or dishes, that stack on top of each other, so that the hot food can be put in each level, each item separate from the others, and then stacked on top of each other so that they all keep each other warm. Then the whole arrangement locks together with rings at the top that make a place for the chopsticks, which fit into a little slot on the side and hold the whole stack together. Once everything is locked in place, you can put it on your bicycle or carry it in your hand or pack it in a tote, and you're all set. And the four dishes hold enough food that four or five people could enjoy sharing the lunch all together.

So let's imagine ourselves having a sisterly lunch and talking about sisterly feelings. Regardless of differences in our ages, our experiences in life, the Church callings we happen to hold right now, or our life circumstances, there are some things we will all need to be willing to do if we are to nourish our sense of shared sisterhood. The first is to honor each other's choices. The second is to not judge each other. The third is to forgive one another. The fourth is to pray. And the fifth is to be of service. Lunch will nourish us for a day or two, but these gifts will build sisterhood for eternity, because they are eternal qualities, and they are also the basis of our relationship with the Savior.

President George Q. Cannon said:

> Our God can be trusted to the very uttermost. No matter how serious the trial, how deep the distress, how great the affliction, He will never desert us. He never has, and He never will. He cannot do it. It is not His character. He is an unchangeable being; the same yesterday, the same today, and He will be the same throughout the eternal ages to come.
>
> We have found that God. We have made Him our friend, by obeying His Gospel; and He will stand by us. We may pass through the fiery furnace; we may pass through deep waters; but we shall not be consumed nor overwhelmed. We shall emerge from all these trials and difficulties the better and purer for them, if we only trust in our God and keep His commandments.
>
> Then He has a future for us. That bliss which we have a foretaste of here, we shall have a fulness of hereafter. You who have received the Holy Spirit; you who have felt its power; you whose hearts have been gladdened under its heavenly influence, you know how sweet it has been; you know that there is nothing on earth so sweet as the out-pouring of the Spirit of God on a human being. No matter what experience you may have had in riches and in all that earth desires, there is nothing that compares with the heavenly sweetness and joy of the Spirit of God. This is a foretaste of that which is to come. We shall receive a fulness of that, if we are faithful. If we hold on without flinching, and without turning to the right hand or to the left, our God will lead us straight on until we are brought into His presence and crowned with glory, immortality and eternal life.[1]

In other words, if we know how to nourish each other with the bread of eternal life, it is because the Savior has already nourished us, in fact, has made himself the bread of eternal life so that we might never hunger or thirst.

## Honoring Each Other's Choices

Let's see what's in the first tray. Mmm, delicious, carefully prepared crab cakes and cucumber. I'm going to compare this dish to our greatest possession—our moral agency. Technically, it's not a gift. It's an inherent part of our divine nature. Elder Delbert L. Stapley explained, "The children of God were endowed with freedom of choice while yet but spirit beings. The divine plan provided that they be freeborn in the flesh and become heirs to the inalienable birthright of liberty to choose and act for themselves in mortality. It was essential for their eternal progression that they be subjected to the influences of both good and evil."[2]

The entire plan of salvation is organized so that our moral agency will be honored and protected. God will not deprive us of choice, and the war in heaven was waged to ensure our agency. Heavenly Father represents a perfect example of two perfect qualities in perfect balance: he loves us completely, and he respects our agency completely. Obviously the lessons that we are here on the earth to learn are related to these same two qualities. Yet all too often, in our attempts to love someone more perfectly, we end up trying to deprive them of agency. And sometimes our efforts to respect someone's agency make us seem unloving and cold.

If we examine the scriptures, we see how the Lord respects our agency by allowing us to make decisions even while he assures us of his love and makes clear what he himself wishes. Jerrie Hurd, a woman who has carefully studied the stories of women mentioned in the scriptures, has written:

> Often when revelation needed to be communicated regarding young children, babes, or a child yet to be born, the mothers received the information first, and then later

the fathers received a confirmation. This is not a pattern
that holds true for older children—those probably over the
age of twelve—but it is true of young children in example
after example. In other words, the ancients not only held
motherhood as sacred but also a woman's decisions concerning young children and childbearing. The most obvious
example concerns Mary the Mother of the Savior. An angel
appeared and told her she would be the most blessed woman
among women. [But] Mary had to give her consent even to
this great honor. . . . The Lord never assumes; he always asks.
The choice is up to the woman (p. 124). [Only] later Joseph
was told not to fear taking Mary as his wife.

An angel also appeared to a woman known only as
Manoah's wife. The angel promised her a child and then
asked her to live as a Nazarite, not drinking wine or any
strong drink and not eating any unclean thing, that her child
might be known as a Nazarite from the womb. The angel further instructed her to never allow a razor to touch her child's
hair, explaining that his hair would be the source of his great
strength. Her child, of course, was to be the Israelite cham-
pion Samson. . . . [Now, please notice that] when Manoah's
wife was asked by an angel to give up certain foods and
strong drink, . . . she was given a choice (p. 124).

Manoah's wife agreed to follow the instructions of the
angel. Then with great happiness she went and told her husband. He prayed that he might also be instructed, and the
Lord answered the father's prayer again by sending an angel
to the woman (Judges 13:9). At this second visitation, the
woman asks the angel to wait while she goes and gets her
husband. When they are both present, the angel confirms
the instructions he had previously given the wife.

Hagar, Sarah's bondwoman, is another good example of a
mother who received the revelation she needed to guide her

child's life. In fact, Hagar received revelation for her son even after he had grown to an age when the father usually took over, but by that time she had been sent away, divorced from Abraham's household, and left to rear her child alone (Gen. 21:17–21). Given those circumstances she seems to have assumed the role of both father and mother in receiving divine direction. An angel appears to Hagar and tells her how to save the child, who was very likely over the age of twelve, and tell her what blessing will come to the child—usually patriarchal privileges. Also Genesis 21:21 states, "and his mother took him a wife out of the land of Egypt"—a role usually played by the father.

There are other examples of women receiving revelation about the birth or rearing of their young children. Jochebed, Moses' mother, took such care in the construction of the basket she launched onto the river, she must have had faith that her plan would succeed. Joseph Smith suggests that Pharaoh's daughter was inspired or divinely appointed to be the young child's protector (JST Gen. 50:29).

There is one notable exception to this pattern—the angel announcing the birth of John the Baptist to his father, Zacharias, as he officiated in the temple. But later Elisabeth, John's mother, is filled with the Holy Ghost at the sound of her cousin Mary's salutation and knows that Mary is carrying the Lord. Who knows what revelation Elisabeth might have received concerning her own child? Perhaps the incident in the temple with Zacharias was the confirmation, not the announcement.[3]

Well, we don't know, of course, but if the Lord scrupulously observed the agency of these women in these scriptural accounts, then don't you think that he feels just as strongly about preserving our own right to choose? The message to me is that we should not quickly or easily surrender our moral agency to any one or to any thing. These women knew what they wanted: Manoah's wife wanted a baby. Jochebed wanted to preserve the life of her child. The Lord responded to their heartfelt prayers, not by saying, "Okay, here it is, you asked for it," but by communicating, "I will grant your desire, if you choose to accept this gift."

When it comes to the choices that we must make, we have literally dozens. What's right in one situation could be exactly the wrong thing in another situation. Discipline that gets one child's attention may turn off another one. What's right for one season of our life may be wrong for another season. Furthermore, often our choices are not between good and evil—that's easy—but between many good options. That's more difficult.

Sisters, I have two requests for you that will nourish you where moral agency is concerned. First, be grateful for the power to choose. You may wish sometimes that your choices were easier or even that someone would make your decisions for you. Although such a wish may be natural, I believe that it is a terrible temptation that we must resist at all costs. Instead of fearing our choices or desiring not to choose, could I ask you instead to thank God for the right and privilege of choice? You will feel freer to ask for the counsel and advice of others when you know that the final decision is yours. You will be more calm when you receive conflicting counsel, or even if someone puts pressure on you to make a certain choice. Know that it is your right to ask God for help and light and that, even if you make a mistake, he will help make it right.

The second request is that you show the same respect for each other's agency. Be supportive, not prescriptive of each other. If someone trusts you enough to ask for your advice, think about it prayerfully and give it gently. Listen more than you talk, pray for her more than you preach at her, and provide loving support before, during, and after her decision. If she has made a mistake, surely she will be able to correct it more swiftly and with less pain if she does not have to face being scolded or have to listen to "I told you so."

So that's the nourishing item in the first tray.

## Withholding Judgment

Now, from the second tray, I want to unpack a generous and richly flavored morsel—let's call it chicken teriyaki—which I am identifying as withholding judgment. We've all grown up with the Savior's instructions, given during the Sermon on the Mount:

> Judge not, that ye be not judged.
>
> For with what judgment ye judge, ye shall be judged: and with what measure ye mete, it shall be measured to you again.
>
> And why beholdest thou the [speck] that is in thy [sister's] eye, but considerest not the [wood chip] that is in thine own eye?
>
> Or how wilt thou say to thy [sister], Let me pull out the [speck] out of thine eye; and, behold, a [wood chip] is in thine own eye? (Matthew 7:1–4.)

We all know that the Savior will eventually stand to judge the living and the dead at the end of the world—in fact, that a final scene regarding this earth's mortal existence will be the Day of Judgment, but while he was here in mortality, he said, "If any [one] hear my words, and believe not, I judge [her] not: for I came not to judge the world, but to save the world" (John 12:47). So judgment will eventually come, but the work of salvation comes first and it requires us not to judge.

I am so grateful for the commandment not to judge. It relieves me of such an enormous and unwelcome burden of appraising, of evaluating, of labeling, of reproaching, and of criticizing. We don't have to approve of our neighbor's politics or religious observances. We don't have to evaluate the parenting style or the homemaking skills of a sister. We don't have to decide whether someone is following the prophet with sufficient rigor. We don't have to look around Relief Society when we enter our meetings and label who is appropriately dressed or who should have taken her baby to the nursery or who is likely to make a comment in class that we won't agree with. We can just sit down next to the first sister that we come to, greet her with love and acceptance, help her if we see a need, and enjoy the spirit of sisterhood during the lesson with her.

A sister from Oregon shared with me a talk she had given in Relief Society about the importance of understanding differences. She used her own life as an example, and it must have been one of the most engaging and memorable lessons that Relief Society had ever had. She and her husband were converts, drawn to the Church because they wanted their children to have a religious experience. They were impressed by the family orientation of Mormonism and were baptized just before Christmas in 1989. She writes:

> Little did we realize what exactly we had gotten into! It was a complete lifestyle change for us! I still feel like a baby—a newborn in the Church. I had such a tough time because I felt so different from everyone. I came from a very different background than *most,* not all, but *most* members. I came from a broken home in which no one believed in a God.

Now ask yourself if you would have found charity and acceptance in your heart for this sister. Her mother was an alcoholic and a drug abuser. She describes her father as "horribly abusive." She left home on the day she was eighteen, but by then she had already experimented with drugs, alcohol, and promiscuity. Sisters, would you be able to love someone from that background? Could you have love and acceptance, even if you didn't understand everything?

I think most of us would feel compassion and want to help her, but I think we might lack understanding. We might think, *Well, that's a terrible background. How fortunate she is to have found the gospel. Of course she'll want to completely change herself and her personality right away.* We might not understand that she *couldn't* change who she is right away. We might not be able even to understand that she might not *want* to change everything about herself immediately. Can you understand that she might just want to be accepted for who and what she is? And then, in the safe space of that acceptance and love, begin to change herself?

Acceptance doesn't mean approval of her former lifestyle and personality. It means loving her *eternal* self and having faith in the gospel that she can and will change because that eternal self will desire righteousness and be drawn to it. She goes on to say:

> When I joined the Church, I was completely overwhelmed. I felt completely different from everyone! I hated crafts and baking, I didn't particularly enjoy being a mother, and I wasn't perfect! You see, I perceived everyone in the Church to be perfect and to have perfect lives. This was detrimental to me for I became discouraged and severely depressed. I felt stifled in such a homogenous atmosphere! I thought that I must have been the only Democrat in the whole church; I certainly was the only one who swore up a blue streak when I stubbed my toe; and I definitely knew that I was the only mother who wanted to do bodily harm to my children on a fairly regular basis.

So she did a perfectly natural thing. She stopped coming to church. Now, what she didn't know is that she wasn't all that different from the rest of us. Periods of inactivity are actually not all that exceptional in the Church, even for people who are lifetime members—who are born to Mormon parents and baptized at age eight. According to a study done by the Research and Evaluation Department for the Church, "about 75 percent of lifelong Latter-day Saints experience a period of inactivity lasting a year or more."

About 60 percent of them eventually come back.[4] That suggests that we should have a lot of understanding and no harsh judgments for people who feel so uncomfortable at church that they don't feel they can come. Most of them will eventually respond to our acceptance. And this sister was the same. She wrote:

> While away from the Church, I had fun. I'm not going to lie to you. It was a sense of freedom to me, a release from all of the incredible guilt that I had been feeling. After months, seven to be exact, I decided that I had better go back to church because I was worried about the kids missing out on church. I went back haughty and rebellious. I had been unintentionally hurt by a few people, and I was very different, but I was going to show everyone that I was . . . proud of it!!

Can we understand how she felt? She had felt judged and it had hurt. But for her children's sake—not even for the sake of her own spirituality—she was ready to try again. She could see and feel something that she wanted for her children, and she hoped she could be accepted just for herself. She describes her own mellowing, how she tried not to judge others, not even those who hurt her feelings. She accepted them as having acted unintentionally and without personal malice toward her. But she also came to accept herself as she was—imperfect and struggling, but worthwhile and making progress. Her closing message is:

> I don't want you to think that this is a perfect and happy ending, because it's not. Every day is a struggle for me. A struggle not to swear, a struggle to pray, a struggle not to smoke my cigarettes, a struggle to deal righteously with my children, and a struggle to come to church on Sundays. But I'm taking it day by day: little bit by little bit; person by person; and situation by situation.

I do love Jesus and his gospel and I know he died for my
sins, so there's always hope.[5]

Now, when we understand how hard she is trying, our hearts go
out to her in love and support, don't they? My dear sisters, we never
know enough to judge anyone. Only God does. We just need to
accept them, love them, share our faith with them, and serve them
as best we can. One of the most important things we can share is the
great joy and gladness that the gospel gives us. The gospel is good
news, not bad news. And it came to us because we are imperfect and
we need it to help us be better, not because we are perfect and have
no room to improve. The Savior loves each one of us, even in our
imperfections. He wants us all to be righteous, but each person has
her own pathway toward being righteous. That's why we are given
the gift of the Holy Ghost, so that we can receive guidance as we
follow our individual paths.

## Serve One Another

Now, as I open the third tray, imagine that it's tempura vegetables. I want to compare this tasty dish to service. I have to chuckle
every time I think of the prayer of a very honest sister who peti-
tioned, "Dear Lord, I ask not for a faith that will move a mountain
but for a faith that will somehow move me."[6] Can you relate to that
prayer? I certainly can!

Yet sometimes I think that we create difficulties for ourselves
because we think of service as projects and jobs, as something
complicated and elaborate and long-term. I'd like us to think of it
rather as a simple sharing of what we have and what we know. How
many of you know how to balance a checkbook? A lack of knowledge of how to perform simple math functions like addition and
subtraction keep many ambitious and entrepreneurial women in
Third World countries from being able to tell if someone is cheating
them. How many of you have a sewing machine? In some countries,
this possession means that you would have the means of earning a

living for yourself. How many of you can use a computer? (I'm counting myself, even though I'm far from skilled.) Sisters, there are many skills that we take completely for granted, yet there are others whose lives are darker and harder because they lack these skills.

The nourishing message from this layer of the sisterly lunchbox is that what you have to share is enough. It is needed. It will comfort and help if it is offered with love.

For example, in one family when the mother died after a devastating illness, a neighbor named Brother Anderson immediately came to the home and offered to help. The daughter, Linda, heard her father thank him but say everything was taken care of.

But Brother Anderson was emphatic:

"You don't understand. I want to help. What can I do?" He stood there silently as Dad again assured him that he couldn't think of anything. Then the man said something to my father I've never forgotten: "Let me have your shoes." Dad looked surprised.

"What do you want with my shoes, Clark?" he asked.

"You'll be pretty busy the next few days, and I know how to put a nice shine on your dress shoes. Please let me shine your shoes."

With tears in his eyes, Dad returned from the bedroom with his dress shoes in hand. "You really don't need to do this, Clark," Dad said, handing the man his shoes.

"Yes, I do," Clark answered.

Within a few hours, Brother Anderson returned with Dad's shined shoes. Dad chuckled as he thanked him for the favor, almost embarrassed that someone had helped in such a personal way. "Now let me have your other shoes," Brother Anderson said.

Again puzzled, Dad asked, "What for?"

"Well, you'll need a shine on the others to match this pair."

Reluctantly, Dad brought out his other shoes and gave them to Brother Anderson. The next day, the shoes were returned, so well polished you could see yourself in the reflection.[7]

You may not think that shining shoes is a very vital skill or a very important service, but that neighbor's service comforted that husband's grieving heart and gave the daughter an example of loving, generous service that she has never forgotten. So when I say that what you have to share is enough, and that the service you offer in love is a blessing, please remember the shining shoes. Jesus promised that those who offer "a cup of cold water only in the name of a disciple, verily I say unto you, [she] shall in no wise lose [her] reward" (Matthew 10:42).

When a little girl was frightened in the night, her father consoled her and explained that God is always with us. "I know God is always here," she replied, squeezing his hand. "But sometimes I need his touch with some skin on it."[8] Well, sisters, we're the skin that often lets His hands touch others.

## The Power of Prayer

In the fourth tray of our Japanese lunchbox is rice, the essential ingredient in a well-balanced Japanese or Chinese meal. In our analogy the rice stands for prayer, the thing that holds everything else together. For prayer connects us to the love of God and of Jesus Christ in the same way that plugging a lamp into the wall socket connects us with the source of power that gives the lamp a reason to exist and that makes the bulb in it light up. Sisters, we have nothing to give if we do not have this vital connection to the Lord. This is why, in my opinion, the Apostle Paul and the prophet Mormon both say that charity is the pure love of Christ, for which we should fervently pray with all "energy of heart." Because nothing else counts if love is lacking. We can speak the language of angels. We can have the gift of prophecy. We can possess all knowledge and have faith so great we can move mountains and give away everything we possess and even become martyrs for our faith, but without love, we are no more than the sound of a bell or a cymbal that attracts attention for a few seconds but then dies away on the air (see 1 Corinthians 13:1–3; Moroni 7:44–48).

I truly believe that we have no hope of possessing that love unless we know by direct revelation from the Holy Ghost how much our Father in Heaven and our Savior Jesus Christ love us. And then if we know their love, there is no way that we can be prevented from having that love spill out of our own hearts to nurture and nourish everyone we come in contact with.

Remember how we began this chapter by marveling at the balance that our Heavenly Father keeps between moral agency and love? Prayer is what helps maintain that balance. We exercise our agency when we choose to pray so that God can do his work of love in us, bless us, teach us, support us as we go through adversity, and still honor our agency. I wonder sometimes what blessings we might be denying ourselves because we do not pray for them with faith and trust and love.

And the second point I want to make about prayer is that it is also the golden balance that allows us, imperfect and immature and unwise as we are, to show a combination of love and respect for the agency of others. No prayer is ever wasted. In the economy of heaven, each prayer has its place. Each prayer has its answer. And I truly believe that we do not even begin to understand how eagerly our prayers are listened to and how willingly they are answered.

Let me close with one final story about prayer. Dr. Larry Dossey was doing his medical residency in Dallas when he treated his first cancer patient, a man with a malignancy that had spread through both his lungs. He had few treatment options and decided to have none, yet every time Dr. Dossey stopped by his room, the man was surrounded by visitors from his church, singing and praying. A year later when Dr. Dossey was working at another hospital, a colleague casually told Dr. Dossey that his former patient was still alive and asked if he wanted to see the man's chest X rays. They were completely clear. There was no sign of cancer. But he had received no treatment—unless you count prayer.

Many years later, Dr. Dossey came across a rigid, double-blind study that had been done by a cardiologist at San Francisco General Hospital. Half of a group of cardiac patients were prayed for and half were not. Those who were prayed for did significantly better. But neither the patients, nurses, nor doctors knew which group the patients were in. It stunned Dr. Dossey. He said, "If the technique being studied had been a new drug or a surgical procedure instead of prayer, it would have been heralded as some sort of breakthrough."

He began looking for other studies and found more than 100 experiments that met scientific standards. Now he researches the connection between prayer and health full time. He has come to five conclusions:

1. The power of prayer does not diminish with distance and exists outside of time. It is just as effective to pray for someone thousands of miles away as it is to pray for someone at their bedside.

2. Prayer can be continuous. To a prayerful person, an attitude of prayerfulness can continue even when doing other activities or even while he or she is asleep. Dr. Dossey quoted a spiritual leader known as Isaac the Syrian who said, "When the Spirit has come to reside in someone, that person cannot stop praying; for the Spirit prays without ceasing in him."

3. There is no right or wrong way to address God. You can say a memorized prayer or pray spontaneously, although apparently those who offer personalized prayers don't give up as quickly.

4. The best kind of prayer is not a specific list of instructions to God but a plea that leaves the method of providing the miracle up to God. Dr. Dossey pointed out that it can be quite bewildering, in dealing with a specific health problem, to know whether you should pray for an increase or decrease of blood flow to a specific organ, for

an increase or a decrease in a specific type of blood cell. Prayers of relinquishment, such as "thy will be done" may seem like giving up to some people, but they actually seem to work best.

5. Love increases the power of prayer. He told about the tangible power of this love. One survey of 10,000 men with heart disease found a 50 percent reduction in frequency of chest pain among married men who perceived their wives as supportive and loving.

Then he told this story about a miracle. A boy had nursed a wounded pigeon back to health and given it an identification tag. The next winter, the boy became ill and was rushed to a hospital two hundred miles away. While he was recovering, a pigeon tapped at the window and, when a nurse opened it, flew in. It was the boy's pigeon, the identification tag still in place. The bird had never been to this place before. Dr. Dossey confessed his ignorance as to how such things are possible and concluded with the final characteristic of prayer: it reminds us that we are not alone and connects us to "that part of us that is infinite in space and time."[9]

Sisters, you do not know what miracles you may help happen if you are willing to pray for yourself and for others.

## Conclusion

Sisters, dear sisters, I invite you to reach out to strengthen your sisterly connections. Break bread with each other, literally and figuratively, and always have a prayer in your heart that the Savior will also be your guest at such loving lunches. He will, for he has promised, "Where two or three are gathered together in my name, there am I in the midst of them" (Matthew 18:20).

Now, a Japanese style lunch may not be entirely to your liking, but find the spiritual and emotional food that will nurture those in your circle of sisters, including these key ingredients:

First, honor each other's choices. Remember the stories of Mary, of Samson's mother, of Hagar and Elizabeth. Remember that God himself waits for us to ask before bestowing a blessing.

Second, let's refrain from judging. Think about the woman from Oregon who was struggling to overcome the effects of an abusive upbringing and her own experiments with drugs, alcohol, and promiscuity. Be part of an accepting, welcoming environment where others can work toward change without having to deal with the additional pain caused by rejection and condemnation.

Third, think of service. And remember, the everyday, ordinary skills that we have to offer, even the ability to give a pair of shoes a good shine, are enough if they are given with love and prompted by a desire to help.

And fourth, draw upon the miracle of prayer—our connection to God and the source of all our strength.

I ask our Heavenly Father that we might follow the counsel given by Apostle Paul to the Saints of his day and receive the promised blessing:

> Rejoice in the Lord alway: and again I say, Rejoice. . . .
>
> Be [worried about] nothing; but in every thing by prayer and supplication with thanksgiving let your requests be made known unto God.
>
> And the peace of God, which passeth all understanding, shall keep your hearts and minds through Christ Jesus. (Philippians 4:6–7.)

# 9

# LIVING WATER

$\mathcal{I}$ love the gospel. I love to learn about it. I love to think about it. I love to share my testimony about it. In this chapter I'd like to explore with you some thoughts about the living water of the gospel and what it means to draw that living water from the well.

You remember that Jesus used the phrase "living water" when he spoke to the Samaritan woman at the well—the first recorded person to whom he testified of his divinity. When she was surprised that he, a man, would speak to her, a woman, and even more surprised that he, a Jew, would speak to her, a Samaritan, asking her for a drink, "Jesus answered and said unto her, If thou knewest the gift of God, and who it is that saith to thee, Give me to drink; thou wouldest have asked of him, and he would have given thee living water" (John 4:10).

Why was she surprised at the exchange? Because two barriers stood between him and her—the social restrictions of gender and race. Alas, they are still barriers in parts of our society today, sometimes even within the Church.

But what many of us seem to miss is the fact that what should have been the greatest barrier of all simply did not exist for Jesus any more than these first two barriers did. This woman was a sinner, a mortal human being with imperfections and weaknesses. Jesus was God and the Son of God, sinless, stainless, and perfect. This difference in their natures should have been a barrier that made them

different species to each other, unapproachable, incomprehensible—
like a lion and a lily. But because of Jesus' love for us, our different
natures are not a barrier. He wants to give us his nature so that holiness and divinity and love will spring up within us like living water.

The Savior said something stirring and profound to Joseph Smith
when he gave him this promise:

> And now, verily I say unto you, that as I said that I would
> make known my will unto you, behold I will make it known
> unto you, not by the way of commandment, for there are
> many who observe not to keep my commandments.
>
> But unto him that keepeth my commandments I will
> give the mysteries of my kingdom, and the same shall be in
> him a well of living water, springing up unto everlasting life.
> (D&C 63:22–23.)

The mysteries of the kingdom are the mysteries of the King.
Understanding the mysteries means understanding the mystery of
how, as the prophet Abinadi said, "God himself should come down
among the children of men, and take upon him the form of man, and
go forth in mighty power upon the face of the earth" (Mosiah 13:34).
To understand the mysteries is to comprehend the need for and the
saving power of the Atonement. It's grasping the idea of a love so
pure and so profound that Jesus was willing to sacrifice his life for us.
It's treasuring the concept of moral agency and the hope of obtaining
eternal life. Surely, it is this kind of knowledge that constitutes the
living water, which nurtures in us the faith to embrace the gospel of
Jesus Christ, abide by its principles and ordinances, and follow its
teachings as it leads us back into the presence of the Father.

I'd like us to think about the power of living water in three ways.
First, I want us to think about building a living and loving relationship with the Savior. Second, I want us to think about building an
intense appreciation for the scriptures. And third, I want us to think

about how having a living testimony spills over into being a bearer of that testimony in every thought, in every word, in every deed.

## Loving the Savior

Let's begin with loving the Savior. I'm not going to discuss keeping the commandments. I know that you already know the importance of partaking of the sacrament worthily, attending the temple, paying your tithing, fulfilling your responsibilities, and attending your meetings. Any member of the Church knows the commandments and the prerequisites for being worthy, and we could fill a whiteboard with commandments and rules, with should's and ought's, and do's and don'ts.

But remember, the mysteries of the kingdom are the mysteries of its King. Let's go to the foundation beneath all of these laws to the lawgiver, to the Savior himself.

I think that sometimes it is very easy for people to have a relationship with words *about* Jesus without ever having a relationship *with* Jesus. I think that sometimes we become deeply involved with information about him without actually being deeply involved with *him*. We can sometimes live for years on a secondhand relationship with the Lord without even realizing that our hearts are *hungry* for that primary relationship with him and that our souls lack peace because they are anchored somewhere besides in our Savior. We feel *poor* because our treasure is not the Savior's love and mercy for us. We feel *afraid* because we have not felt the assurance of his everlasting arms around us. We feel *powerless* because we have not experienced our will being in harmony with the irresistible force of his plan for the universe.

One of the treasures in the scriptures is the testimonies of the Lord, the outpourings of joy and happiness and gladness and worship and adoration by those who have experienced firsthand what it means to love him and be loved by him. Here is one such beautiful passage from Psalms:

Bless the LORD, O my soul: and all that is within me, bless his holy name.

Bless the LORD, O my soul, and forget not all his benefits:

Who forgiveth all thine iniquities; who healeth all thy diseases;

Who redeemeth thy life from destruction; who crowneth thee with lovingkindness and tender mercies;

Who satisfieth thy mouth with good things; so that thy youth is renewed like the eagle's.

The LORD executeth righteousness and judgment for all that are oppressed.

He made known his ways unto Moses, his acts unto the children of Israel.

The LORD is merciful and gracious, slow to anger, and plenteous in mercy.

He will not always chide: neither will he keep his anger for ever.

He hath not dealt with us after our sins; nor rewarded us according to our iniquities.

For as the heaven is high above the earth, so great is his mercy toward them that fear him. (Psalm 103:1–11.)

This psalm is a remarkable expression of exuberant and joyful love. And did you notice how candidly the singer acknowledged things that normally we scramble to cover up and are humiliated if anyone suggests their presence? Things such as sins and iniquities, a need for healing, and a devastated life. All of these negative things can be acknowledged freely because the psalmist is so filled with joy about the positive things. They overflow his heart with amazement and gratitude and worship.

I was also very interested in the distinction that the psalmist makes when he says that the Lord "made known his ways unto Moses, his acts unto the children of Israel." What is the difference between knowing God's ways and knowing his acts? Well, I'm not sure, but do you remember that when the children of Israel completed their tabernacle in the wilderness, Moses went into the tabernacle, and the pillar of cloud descended on it and filled the doorway "and the LORD talked with Moses." The people stood in their tent doors, worshipping from a respectful distance while "the LORD spake unto Moses face to face, as a man speaketh unto his friend" (Exodus 33:9–11).

I think that verse clarifies the difference. You know someone's ways when you've spent a lot of time with him or her. You know how he or she thinks about things, feels about things, how he or she will react, what's important, what's funny. One commentator on this verse wrote:

> Most Christians would prefer to see God perform mighty miracles rather than to have fellowship with Him and learn His ways. . . . God made known His mighty acts to the people of Israel, but to Moses He "made known His ways." Exodus 33 records a great crisis in which Moses humbly prayed, "If I have found grace in Your sight, show me now Your way." He wanted to know God and His plans for His people more than to see another mighty miracle. No wonder the Lord conversed with him "as a man speaks to his friend" (v. 11). Commenting on the difference between ways and acts, F. B. Meyer wrote, "Ways, or plans, are only made known to the inner circle of the saints; the ordinary congregation learns only His acts."

A talented friend of mine, Jennifer, learned this difference after spending several years in a wheelchair. One day she tearfully prayed, "Lord, I could have done so much for You, if only I could have been healthy." God's response was inaudible but clear: "Many people work for Me, but very few are willing to be My friend."[1]

I invite you to think of the scriptures as love letters and diary entries and notes scribbled on the backs of envelopes and formal proclamations written out with great seals from people who knew the Lord and his ways, who had seen him in action in their lives, and who felt his love reaching out to them and influencing them. What a privilege it is for us to have this wonderful depository of stories about God from people who knew him personally.

But my question to you is this: Do you have the same personal relationship? Do you know Jesus and his ways? Are you writing your own scriptures in your diary and in the testimony that you bear and in the actions of your daily lives? Perhaps you haven't thought of things in quite this way; but if your world is alive with your knowledge of Jesus and your awareness that he exists and that he loves you, then you have a vital, vibrant, living relationship to talk about. Every day there are conversations. Every day there are miracles. Every day there are problems that he helps you solve. Every day there is movement toward healing and wholeness and holiness. This is a record that is personal to you, but it is as eloquent as the Psalms, as dramatic as Moses and the children of Israel, and as tender as the teachings of Jesus.

You may think that you don't know the Savior and that you don't have this kind of relationship with him. I dare say, you may not be conscious of him in your world, but *he* is very conscious of you in *his* world. He loves you. He knows you. He wants you to love him and know him. Begin with the simplest question, "Jesus, are you with me?" Think about him during the day. Let thoughts about Jesus come to your mind with sweetness. Ask him questions. Talk things over with him. Let a running prayer-conversation fill your life with the sound of living water.

If you will do this, I promise that you will have plenty to say about Jesus and plenty to testify of Jesus. Think how ironic it would be if someone came to you and asked, "Tell me about your mother?" And all you could say was, "Well, I don't know what to say, but I have a letter from my sister about her. Let me read that to you." Or if your daughter asked, "How did you meet Dad? When did you know you loved him and wanted to marry him?" What if you could only say, "You know, I can't remember. But I think I have a memo somewhere telling me how he likes his eggs and how to iron his shirts." Wouldn't that be strange? Wouldn't that be sad?

Jesus yearns for us to know him. He told his disciples, "If a man love me, he will keep my words: and my Father will love him, and we will come unto him, and make our abode with him" (John 14:23). We know that this scripture applies to everyone, so let's read it again, rephrasing it a little so that it speaks directly to us here: "If you love me, you will keep my words: and my Father will love you, and we will come unto you, and make our abode with you." And to Joseph Smith in our own day, the Savior said: "Verily, thus saith the Lord: It shall come to pass that every soul who forsaketh his [or her] sins and cometh unto me, and calleth on my name, and obeyeth my voice, and keepeth my commandments, shall see my face and know that I am" (D&C 93:1).

Jesus doesn't just want us to know *about* him. He wants us to know *him.*

Commenting on the remarkable experience had by the brother of Jared, whose faith was so great that the Savior showed himself to this prophet, Elder Jeffrey R. Holland has written:

> This may be one of those provocative examples (except that here it is a real experience and *not* hypothetical) a theologian might cite in a debate about God's power. Students of religion sometimes ask, "Can God make a rock so heavy that he cannot lift it?" or "Can God hide an item so skillfully that he cannot find it?" Far more movingly and importantly one may ask here, "Is it possible to have faith so great that even God cannot resist it?" At first one is inclined to say that surely God could block such an experience if he wished to. But the text suggests otherwise: "This man . . . *could not*

*be kept from beholding within the veil. . . . He could not be kept from within the veil."*

This may be an unprecedented case of a mortal man's desire, will, and purity so closely approaching the heavenly standard that God could not but honor his devotion. What a remarkable doctrinal statement about the power of a mortal's faith! And not an ethereal, unreachable, select mortal, either. This was a man who once forgot to call upon the Lord, one whose best ideas were sometimes focused on rocks, and one who doesn't even have a traditional name in the book that has immortalized his unprecedented experience. Given such faith, we should not be surprised that the Lord would show this prophet much, show him visions that would be relevant to the mission of all the Book of Mormon prophets and to the events of the latter-day dispensation in which the book would be received.[2]

Even if we know the scriptures well, we will only know *about* Jesus if we don't have a primary relationship with him. When we know Jesus himself, then the scriptures come alive for us.

## Love the Scriptures

Let's explore the second point: loving the scriptures. I've already suggested you think of the scriptures as though they are love letters from people who know Jesus personally. When you also know the Savior, then you will be eager to talk to others who know him, just as you are eager to talk about the people you love with other people you love.

You will not have to drag yourself to scripture study or find yourself reluctant to pick up the scriptures. You will hurry to them eagerly because they contain news of the Savior, whom you love, and you will find yourself entering into a joyous dialogue with the scriptures, saying, "Yes! I know exactly how that feels!" and "I have had the same blessing" and "God is so good to me."

A few years ago when I visited a Relief Society conference in Michigan, I was thrilled by the gift of a book of testimonies that the sisters prepared for me. Sister Marie Whitaker of Sterling Heights in Bloomfield Hills Stake wrote about the great love for the Book of Mormon that she acquired during the year she was called to be stake education counselor and had oversight of the then new literacy program. Although she had long loved the Book of Mormon, she now found that "the Lord taught me new things and gave me experiences that allowed me to see how to apply the scriptures to my life in giving me strength, inspiration, and comfort."

When she was released a few months later and called to serve as a ward Relief Society president, she saw a great need among the sisters for the strength and comfort that had come to her. With the cooperation of the local institute teacher, a class was sponsored. Twenty women began meeting together weekly to discuss five or ten chapters in detail and to share their testimonies with each other. Sister Whitaker writes, "Those who have come have grown in testimony, have experienced, for the first time in some cases, the scriptures opening up to them, answering questions pertaining to their life and those in their families. I rarely went to a class that the Lord did not show me how to handle a problem either of great concern in my life or in the life of a sister I was praying about."[3]

Think about coming indoors when you've been working outside or you've taken a long walk on a hot summer day. Even if you're not dangerously dehydrated, imagine how eagerly you fill your tallest glass with cool water, maybe add a few ice cubes and swish them around, listening to them chink together as the moisture films the outside of your glass. And then you take that first, delicious gulp. Ahhh! Think how satisfied, comfortable, and refreshed you feel by the time you've finished.

As I was thinking about wells and fountains of living water, I remembered a terrible accusation that the Lord brought against the people of Israel, which is recorded in Jeremiah. The Savior says: "For my people have committed two evils; they have forsaken me the fountain of living waters, and hewed them out cisterns, broken cisterns, that can hold no water" (Jeremiah 2:13). So not only had they turned from the good, but they had actually constructed substitutes—cheap, broken substitutes, substitutes that can't even pretend to do the job right. The people had not only been disobedient and unloving and ungrateful, but they had also been hypocrites, pretending that their broken cisterns could hold living water when they could hold nothing but spiders and drifting sand from the desert.

In contrast is the testimony of Peter, expressed at a time when many of the disciples had turned away from Jesus, feeling that his gospel was too demanding and no longer willing to believe in him: "Then said Jesus unto the twelve, Will ye also go away? Then Simon Peter answered him, Lord, to whom shall we go? thou hast the words of eternal life. And we believe and are sure that thou art that Christ, the Son of the living God" (John 6:66–69).

Peter knew the taste of living water. He was not willing to accept any substitute. He understood that it was a matter of spiritual life and death for him.

In the convenience of our world, we're used to turning on a faucet and having water right there, literally at our fingertips. We think of it as "our" water, as though the well were in our basements. It's easy for us to forget that it comes to us in pipes from distant reservoirs. Most of us have no idea where our water even comes from. The Samaritan woman knew where her water came from because she had to go to the well for it. It might have been more convenient for her to build her house around the well, but that wasn't an option. Instead, she had to go to where the water was then take away what she could carry so that she would have it for her use.

We're in a similar situation. The scriptures are a deep well, flowing with the testimonies of those who have had personal experiences with our Heavenly Father and Jesus. There is more water than we can ever use. Our personal testimonies are like the well of living water promised us by the Savior, springing up within us inexhaustibly and abundantly, so much that we need never worry about running out. But at the same time, we are mortal. We are imperfect. We all have sins to be repented of and things that we can do better. There are desert times for all of us. Dry times. Thirsty times. Times when we realize that what we thought was a well is in fact a broken cistern—often a cistern that we have hewed out with our own hands. At such times, a sip of cool water can remind us of what we need. It can give us enough strength to turn around and go back to the well.

Remember this physical feeling, and then remember the spiritual feelings of drinking living water. Remember the love Jesus has for you and his longing that you come to know him as he knows you.

President Gordon B. Hinckley has testified:

> I am grateful for [the] emphasis on reading the scrip-tures. I hope that for you this will become something far more enjoyable than a duty; that, rather, it will become a love affair with the word of God. I promise you that as you read, your minds will be enlightened and your spirits will be lifted. At first it may seem tedious, but that will change into a wondrous experience with thought and words of things divine.[4]

This is my testimony as well. When we love the Savior, we will love the scriptures, and they in turn will increase our love for the Savior.

## Love and Service

And that brings us to the third point: Once our lives are con-nected to the Savior and to the scriptures, then love for others will rise up easily and spontaneously—like a fountain—into our lives, and we will find ourselves gratefully serving as Jesus served, eagerly speaking of Jesus, reverently testifying of Jesus. When our hearts are filled with gratitude for the mercies of Christ and for his loving kindness to us, how can we do anything but feel an overflowing concern and love for those who also need the same source of joy and reassurance and strength in their lives? How can we do anything but desire to serve them and meet their needs?

The Prophet Joseph Smith understood this concept. He observed, "Love is one of the chief characteristics of Deity, and ought to be manifested by those who aspire to be the sons of God. A man [or woman] filled with the love of God, is not content with blessing his [or her] own family alone, but ranges through the whole world, anxious to bless the whole human race."[5]

I have a little gift that a friend gave me a couple of years ago, something that he'd made in his wood shop and painted himself.

The friend who gave me this sign is Jack Anderson. He was a missionary in Hawaii whom I met when I was a student at the University of Hawaii during the 1940s. He was from Salt Lake City, and when my husband and I moved to Utah in the early 1950s, we found him teaching band in high school.

A couple of years ago, I spoke in his ward. He came up afterward, shook hands with me, and visited with me for a few minutes. Then he gave me a little object made out of wood. I said, "Oh, it's very pretty. Thank you very much."

But I had a puzzled look on my face, and he smiled. He said, "There's a message in it, but I won't tell you about it right now. Call me if you can't figure it out."

Well, I couldn't figure it out. I wondered if it was Korean, because Korean characters are quite angular and geometric. I wondered if it was some kind of ancient rune. But I wasn't going to call Jack. I was going to figure it out. It took about three weeks. I put it in the kitchen and looked at it every day. I held it close. I held it far away. I looked and looked and just couldn't make sense of it.

I finally put the woodcut on the ledge of my kitchen window.

The next morning, I was leaving the house and talking to myself—the way I do since my husband died. I said, "Goodbye, house!" and glanced back at the kitchen window. The word *Jesus* sprang out of the sign at me so suddenly and so vividly that it actually startled me.

I went back, picked it up, and laughed and laughed. What had been so puzzling to me was now so very clear. I called Jack and said, "It took me a long time, but I finally got it!" And we laughed together.

I still have this sign on the ledge above my kitchen sink. Every time I look at it, I think about Jack and about the affection he had for Ed and me and about his kindness in giving me this little memento of his own faith and love for the Savior. I think about how my testimony and Jack's testimony give us something in common because we both love the same Savior.

A couple of summers ago, I kept hearing very faint noises in my house at night. I could never find anything out of place or see anything amiss, but the noises puzzled me. Then in early autumn I noticed a little debris on the hearth of the living room fireplace and one of my friends suggested that it might be a raccoon in the chimney. So I called a chimney cleaning company and they sent someone out.

Sure enough, a raccoon had found a way to climb down the chimney and make a nest in the space between the firewall and the outside bricks of the chimney. Not only that, she had raised a family there! I seldom use the fireplace in the living room, but I frequently build a fire in the family room, and its fireplace backs up to the one in the living room. So this furry family was lucky it was summer and I hadn't had a fire there for three or four months. By the time I had figured out what the problem was and called the company, she had raised the babies and showed them how to climb out of the chimney and set off on their adventures.

Wouldn't that have been a sight! A mother raccoon and three or four babies crawling out of my chimney on a night with a full moon, climbing down the side of the house or jumping into one of the trees that grows close to the roofline, and then setting off across the neighborhood. No wonder the dogs bark at night!

Anyway, the man from the company was very professional and competent. He'd seen many cases like this before. He explained to me how raccoons can do things like this. He cleaned and sanitized the space so that if the raccoons had left any mites or insects there, they wouldn't be a problem. He installed a guard over the top of the chimney so that there wouldn't be any more furry or feathery trespassers. He was very businesslike in all that he did. As the last thing, he checked the fireplace in the family room to be sure there weren't any problems there. As he straightened up, he looked across the family room into the kitchen and saw this little sign sitting on my window ledge.

"Oh!" he exclaimed, startled. "Are you a Christian?"

"Yes, I am," I said.

It was an immediate bond between us. We talked for a few minutes, with warmth and interest. I told him about Jack and how long it had taken me to see Jesus. He laughed softly, shaking his head ruefully. He knew exactly what I meant. Although we were of different religious faiths, we loved the same Savior, and it made a strong bond between us—based on more than our mutual interest in raccoons.

We didn't know each other, but we loved each other and could teach each other because we both loved Jesus. I know you do not need to be reminded of the importance of rendering compassionate service. I know you do not need to be reminded about the importance of kindness. I know that you know that "Christ cannot live his life today in this world without our mouth, without our eyes, without our going and coming, without our heart. When we love, it is Christ loving through us. This is Christianity."[6]

But sometimes we don't realize that we are always testifying. We are testifying by example. We are testifying about the reality of Christ by the vibrancy of our own faith. We are testifying about honesty and integrity when we live our lives with integrity and speak the truth honestly.

I remember reading about a man named Roy who had been a kidnapper and holdup man for twelve years, until he was caught and imprisoned.

> While in prison he heard the gospel and invited Jesus Christ into his life. [Roy said:] "Jesus said to me, 'I will come and live in you and we will serve this sentence together.' And we did." Several years later he was paroled, and just before he went out he was handed a two-page letter written by another prisoner, which said, "You know perfectly well that when I came into the jail I despised preachers, the Bible, and anything that smacked of Christianity. I went to the Bible class and the preaching service because there wasn't anything else interesting to do.
>
> "Then they told me you were saved, and I said, 'There's another fellow taking the Gospel road to get parole.' But, Roy, I've been watching you for two-and-a-half years. You didn't know it, but I watched you when you were in the yard exercising, when you were working in the shop, when you played, while we were all together at meals, on the way to our cells, and all over, and now I'm a Christian, too, because I watched you. The Savior who saved you has saved me. You never made a slip."
>
> Roy says, "When I got that letter and read it through, I broke out in a cold sweat. Think of what it would have meant if I had slipped, even once."[7]

This convict behind bars was a teacher and a witness for Christ. William Arthur Ward says, "The mediocre teacher tells. The good teacher explains. The superior teacher demonstrates. The great teacher inspires."[8]

Aren't we fortunate? We not only have the greatest subject in the world, but we also have the greatest teacher's aide in the world. The Holy Ghost is with us when we speak the truth about Jesus, because there is no subject more important, no person it is more important for us to encounter, no one who longs more intensely to spend time with us.

## Conclusion

I hope that some of these thoughts have been living water for you. Remember that we explored the importance of first loving the Savior, of having a firsthand relationship with him, not a secondhand relationship where we can only talk about him or pass on the experiences of other people. Remember Moses and the brother of Jared, who talked with God as to a friend, and understand that this is the relationship that the Savior wants with each of us. With you, with me.

We reflected on the importance of loving the scriptures, of seeing them as love letters from other people who knew and loved the Savior just as we do. Remember the woman at the well, taking water to her home. Remember the sound of the ice cube in a glass and the analogy of the first sip of living water refreshing and reviving and keeping us going until we can get back to the well and the fountain of living water that Jesus wants each of us to have, springing up in our hearts. And third, we pondered the importance of loving and serving the people around us, testifying to them of the truth of the gospel through the conduct of our ordinary everyday lives. Think how that task can be easy when it is Christ in us loving that person through us.

In closing, let me remind you of the inspiring blessing that Moses invoked upon his people as he promised them that the love and mercy of God would not fail them:

> I call heaven and earth to record this day . . . that I have set before you life and death, blessing and cursing: therefore choose life, that both thou and thy seed may live:

That thou mayest love the LORD thy God, and that thou mayest obey his voice, and that thou mayest cleave unto him: for he is thy life, and the length of thy days. (Deuteronomy 30:19–20.)

I also testify that Christ *is* our life and our love and the length of our days, for which testimony I am deeply grateful.

# 10

## BEARING THE NAME OF CHRIST

Not long ago, I read this prayer: "So far today, Lord, I've done all right. I haven't gossiped; I haven't lost my temper; I haven't been greedy, grumpy, nasty, selfish, or overindulgent. I'm very thankful for that. But in a few moments, Lord, I'm going to get out of bed. And from then on, I'm going to need a lot of help."[1]

I think we can all relate to this prayer and to this person's experience in the pitfalls of mortality that prompted it. My feeling is that our best preparation for life is to fix our hearts and our faith more firmly on Jesus Christ, our Savior, and that's what I wish to explore in this chapter.

President Gordon B. Hinckley has encouraged us "to cultivate . . . stronger, ever stronger faith in the Lord Jesus Christ, that our people might walk in righteousness and become an example to all and be as the leaven to leaven the lump, as it were. Let us walk in faith and faithfulness."[2]

### The Name of Christ

It is extremely significant that as members of Christ's church we are called to take his name upon us. It is a great privilege to partake of the sacrament each Sunday in company with our brothers and sisters in the gospel. One of the promises we make, which is also a great privilege for us, is to take upon us the name of Jesus Christ, the Savior of the world. Being called by this name changes us. It gives us a new identity. But what exactly does that mean?

Let me give you an example using our own names. Sometimes we think, *I'm just the same old me. Nothing has changed. I've always been this way, and I'll always be this way.* I'd like you to do a little experiment. Get a pencil and a piece of paper and write down the first name of your mother or your grandfather or a good friend, and then write down three adjectives that you associate with that name. For instance, if I were writing down the name of Ken, my oldest son, the three adjectives that come quickly to mind are "kind," "hard-working," and "independent."

Now, think of your own first name or the name or nickname that you go by. Write that down. Now write down three adjectives that you think go with your name, either adjectives that you think fit you or adjectives that you think someone else might use to describe you.

Third, write your name backward. Look at it. How would you pronounce it? What does this name mean to you? You have all kinds of associations and meanings and identity attached to your name spelled frontward—a whole lifetime of knowing who Charles or Deborah or Chieko might be. But who is this other person? My name backwards is O-k-e-i-h-c. I think it's pronounced O-cake. Well, I kind of like that: Oh! *Cake!* Maybe pineapple upside-down cake or German chocolate cake! What kind of adjectives might go with this name? They can be adjectives completely different from those you attach to your frontward name. I think "O-Cake" sounds exciting, exotic, and Irish! How's that for somebody Japanese!

The point, of course, is to say that even little things can help us think differently about ourselves, so who knows what we might discover by thinking a little differently about the idea of taking upon us the name of Christ?

By taking upon us the name of Christ, we become Christians. When Saul was struck down on the road to Damascus, becoming as zealous a convert to Christ as he had been an adversary of Christ, the Savior told Ananias that Paul "is a chosen vessel unto me, to bear my name before the Gentiles, and kings, and the children of Israel" (Acts 9:15).

In much the same way, *we* are chosen to bear his name, to become Christians, to have a Christian identity. In the Book of Mormon, when Alma the Elder was praying about his little flock, baptized at the waters of Mormon, the Lord told him, "Blessed is this people who are willing to bear my name; for in my name shall they be called; and they are mine" (Mosiah 26:18). And now we are called to bear his name and to be Christians.

I was very impressed by a story in the *Church News* that illustrates the importance of having an identity as a Christian. The story was about a German family during the closing days of World War II. The American soldiers had reached their little village and were searching their household. Eleven-year-old Gunther Schlegel had been drilled with the other schoolboys in how to shoot a gun. Someone had given him a rifle and marched him off to guard a local facility; but his father had seen him and pulled him out of the ranks, knowing that the war was over but fearing that his son could still be killed in the battle. The American soldiers had found the gun and were immediately suspicious that someone in the house was a sniper.

The lives of the family members were spared, however, because one soldier from Utah was a Mormon. He saw hanging on a wall in the home a photograph of the Salt Lake Temple and assured his fellow soldiers that the Schlegel family could be trusted.[3]

Think of that. On the strength of that one symbol, which identified them as Mormons, another Mormon was willing to defend this German family to his fellow soldiers—he knew they could be trusted not to be snipers.

But what is the identifying characteristic of a Christian? Some might say it is a cross or the New Testament. But this is how Jesus himself said a Christian could be identified: "A new commandment I give unto you, That ye love one another; as I have loved you, that ye also love one another. [and] By *this* shall all men know that ye are my disciples, if ye have love one to another" (John 13:34–35; emphasis added). Can those around us sense from the way we behave that we are Christians—because we radiate love to others?

As I think about the important lessons we should learn as members of the Church and fellow citizens in the kingdom of God, I hope that first and foremost will be to learn to love the Lord. Second, I hope that you will learn to feel the Savior's love for you. And third, I hope that you will learn to convey that love through humility and service to the people with whom you come in contact.

## Love the Lord

Let's explore the first concept: learning to love the Lord. When Jesus was asked about the most important commandments, he replied in those words we all know and love:

> The first of all the commandments is, Hear, O Israel; The Lord our God is one Lord:
>
> And thou shalt love the Lord thy God with all thy heart, and with all thy soul, and with all thy mind, and with all thy strength: this is the first commandment.
>
> And the second is like, namely this, Thou shalt love thy neighbour as thyself. There is none other commandment greater than these.

But we seldom quote the rest of that scripture, which is the response that the scribe made to him, rephrasing and amplifying what he said. Consider these words:

> And the scribe said unto him, Well, Master, thou hast said the truth: for there is one God; and there is none other but he:
>
> And to love him with all the heart, and with all the understanding, and with all the soul, and with all the strength, and to love his neighbour as himself, is more than all whole burnt offerings and sacrifices.

And . . . Jesus . . . said unto him, Thou art not far from
the kingdom of God. (Mark 12:29–34.)

Being a Jew was a lifestyle as well as a religion. Long lists of
observances governed what the faithful ate and when and how, what
they wore, where they worshipped and how, what they believed,
how they resolved legal disputes, and the language they used in
speaking to each other.

There are observances for these same aspects of life that we also
have as Mormons. There are beverages that we do not consume,
styles of clothing that we do not wear, words that we do not speak,
ceremonies that we participate in, meetings that we go to, books that
we read, books that we don't read, religious considerations in our
political activities, frequent prayers, most of them informal, but a few
very important prayers that must be the same every time they are
spoken.

If we were just making a list of observances, we could go on and
on. But that is not the heart and soul of religion. For the Jews, offering the sacrifices, particularly on the great ceremonial occasions each
year, was the most important religious duty that they had. It was
what set them apart from non-Jews and non-observing Jews.
It was the most important of all the laws that they bound themselves
to obey as a Jew.

What is the parallel for Latter-day Saints? Is it attending the
temple? Is it attending sacrament meeting every week? However we
might define it, if it were possible to draw an exact parallel, Jesus is
saying to us as he said to the Jews, that even more important than
these religious observances is loving God "with all the heart, and
with all the understanding, and with all the soul, and with all the
strength, and to love [our] neighbour as [our]self."

As members of the Church, even if we came from Christian
backgrounds, we are greatly blessed by being in a position to learn to
love the Lord in new ways, in purer ways, in more intense ways.
George Q. Cannon served his first mission to the Hawaiian Islands

in the 1850s. It was not an easy mission. He describes the Hawaiian food called poi, which was made out of the taro root. This particular meal came after Brother Cannon had had nothing to eat but potatoes served without salt and molasses for days on end. The taro had been packed in *ti* leaves and brought to the villages; on the way, it had turned "sour and maggoty," he says. "But the people had cooked it over again, and made it into poi. . . . I ate this poi because it was the best and most palatable food I had tasted for weeks." [p. 34]

He tells this story as an example of how his "bodily wants" had literally been "swallowed up" in his "joy in Christ." [p. 18] He wrote with great power of himself and his fellow missionaries:

> We were willing to live on any food that would sustain our bodies, however common or even disagreeable it might be; we were glad to get a shelter, however humble, to lie under; our desire was to fill our mission; and because we felt thus, the Lord made up for any lack of comfort by giving us His Holy Spirit. I had never been so happy in my life before as I was then. When I prayed, I could go unto God in faith; He listened to my prayers; He gave me great comfort and joy; He revealed Himself to me as He never had done before, and told me that if I would persevere, I should be blessed, be the means of bringing many to the knowledge of the truth, and be spared to return home after having done a good work. Many things were revealed to me, during those days, when He was the only friend we had to lean upon, which were afterwards fulfilled. A friendship was there established between our Father and myself, which, I trust, will never be broken nor diminished, and which I hope has continued to grow stronger from those days to these.[4]

Can we say the same thing: that a friendship is established between us and the Father and between us and the Lord? If there are disagreeable or uncomfortable aspects of our service or our callings, please remember that they can be swallowed up in the joy of learning to love and know God.

One of the most powerful and tender revelations given in our own time was the Lord's revelation to Joseph Smith, recorded in Doctrine and Covenants 84. Jesus Christ himself said: "And again I say unto you, my friends, for from henceforth I shall call you friends . . ." (v. 77). Isn't that a remarkable and tender pledge, coming from the Lord himself? We are in a unique position to claim that powerful relationship, to be a friend to Jesus and to know that he is a friend to us. That section has some particular instructions for missionaries, but his promise is to all of us:

"And any [one] that shall go and preach this gospel of the kingdom, and fail not to continue faithful in all things, shall not be weary in mind, neither darkened, neither in body, limb, nor joint; and a hair of [the] head shall not fall to the ground unnoticed. And [you] shall not go hungry, neither athirst" (v. 80).

Please note that this is a spiritual promise as much as it is a physical one. My husband, Ed, was called to be mission president in Japan. All the time that we served that mission, I rejoiced in the literal fulfillment of this blessing that our minds would not be darkened. We were able to think clearly and rapidly. We could foresee consequences. We could plan effectively and hold steadfastly to what we saw even while we dealt with the unexpected as it came up. I also think that the promise that missionaries "shall not go hungry, neither athirst" is a spiritual promise. There were satisfactions of the Spirit so intense and so long-lasting that we truly felt that we had attended a feast of the Spirit. I know that it is the same for you.

But that is not the end of the promise. Christ renewed to the Saints of this dispensation the identical promise that he had made to his early apostles:

Neither take ye thought beforehand what ye shall say;
but treasure up in your minds continually the words of life,

and it shall be given you in the very hour that portion that shall be meted unto every [one]. . . .

And whoso receiveth you, there I will be also, for I will go before your face. I will be on your right hand and on your left, and my Spirit shall be in your hearts, and mine angels round about you, to bear you up. (D&C 84:85, 88.)

I know that some have received the literal ministration of angels. Let me assure those who have not asked for angels to be round about you or who do not feel that you merit the ministration of angels that this promise is for you, too. The Savior loves you and wants you to learn to love him, too.

## Learn to Feel the Savior's Love for You

So that's the first point. I hope that we will all love the Lord. And second, I hope we will learn to feel the Savior's love for us. Let me share with you the experience of John Murdock, a member of the Church in the 1830s in Kirtland, Ohio. He gave his newborn twins to Joseph and Emma when death took his wife and the Smiths' own newborn twins in the same week. Brother Murdock recorded a vision of the Savior granted to him after he had been taught a particular manner of praying by Joseph Smith. He says:

The visions of my mind were opened and the eyes of my understanding were enlightened, and I saw the form of a man, most lovely. The visage of his face was round and fair as the sun, His hair a bright silver gray, curled in most majestic form; his eyes a keen, penetrating blue, and the skin of his neck a most beautiful white. He was covered from the neck to the feet with a loose garment of pure white—whiter than any garment I had ever before seen. His countenance was most the penetrating, and the most lovely. When the vision was closed up, it left to my mind the impression of love, for months, and I have never before felt it to that degree.[5]

The Savior left an impression of love on this member's mind that lasted for months! Can you imagine the power of that love? And yet that is the kind of love we can convey to others when we have hearts filled with the love of Christ.

John Murdock's experience was extraordinary, but it was not unique, and it should not be unique. The Lord through the prophet Joseph Smith promised a similar experience to every Latter-day Saint who truly desires it. In the first verses of Doctrine and Covenants 93, we read:

> Verily, thus saith the Lord: It shall come to pass that every soul who forsaketh his [or her] sins and cometh unto me, and calleth on my name, and obeyeth my voice, and keepeth my commandments, shall see my face and know that I am;
>
> And that I am the true light that lighteth every [one] that cometh into the world. (D&C 93:1–2.)

The Lord promised the Saints of the latter days the ministration of angels. Now here, in this section, the Lord promises to bless us with a direct face-to-face vision of Him and a sure knowledge that he lives and loves us. Such knowledge is the seal on the faith we have in our hearts that he lives. It takes our testimonies that he lived on this earth, died to effect the atonement of love, and lives still to be our mediator with the Father.

Recall the tremendous prayer of the Apostle Paul in behalf of the early Saints:

> That Christ may dwell in your hearts by faith; that ye, being rooted and grounded in love,
>
> May be able to comprehend with all saints what is the breadth, and length, and depth, and height;

And to know the love of Christ, which passeth knowledge, that ye might be filled with all the fulness of God. (Ephesians 3:17–19)

And remember the promise of Jacob in the Book of Mormon to his people: "O all ye that are pure in heart, lift up your heads and receive the pleasing word of God, and feast upon his love; for ye may, if your minds are firm, forever" (Jacob 3:2).

This is the second message that I hope you'll remember—that the Savior loves you. Feel it. Experience that love. Never doubt it.

## Learn to Convey Love to Others

And third, I hope that, as Christians, we will learn to convey love to others. Elder Lynn A. Mickelsen of the Seventy tells this story:

> When I was twelve years old, we had a community fathers-and-sons banquet in Idaho Falls. President George Albert Smith, the President of the Church, was the speaker. After the banquet, we lined up to shake his hand. When my turn came, President Smith took my hand and spoke to me. I don't remember what he said, but I shall never forget what I felt. From that moment, I wanted to be in the presence of the prophets.
>
> I understand now why I had those feelings. It is not because we worship the prophet. We don't. It is because he is the mouthpiece of the Lord. The prophet is a channel, and through him the Savior's love is projected to the whole world. That channel is open today.
>
> After I was called to be a General Authority, I came early to one of the special meetings in the upper room of the temple. President Ezra Taft Benson was sitting in his place, and as I walked into the room, I looked at him and he looked at me. I wanted to take him in my arms and tell him how

much I loved him, because I could feel *his* love. It was the same kind of love I had felt from President Smith as a twelve-year-old boy. That is why the Saints in South America embrace me and tell me to please give their love to the prophet. They can feel his love even far away. It transcends, or goes beyond, mere miles.[6]

Have you ever been in the presence of someone whose love you could actually feel? An even more humbling question is: Have you ever loved someone with such purity and such intensity that this individual could sense your love without your saying a word?

My prayer is that you will, if you have not already, experience this overwhelming, pure love of Christ for the people you meet and that you will hunger and thirst to teach them the gospel. I pray also that your love will show itself in humility and service.

Let me tell you about my husband. Ed was this kind of a missionary when he was called to preside over the Japan Okinawa Mission in the late 1960s. Japan is a highly structured and hierarchical society, so my husband shocked the members when he walked among them at the first conference, shaking hands and saying, "Okazaki desu. Osewaninarimasu." This means, "I am Okazaki. I am at your service and I place myself under your protection." But the English translation does not convey the full range of emotion that this expression would convey to a Japanese person.

The phrase is an expression that suggests great humility in Japan. It is the phrase that a student would use when coming to learn from a teacher, the phrase an employee would use when presenting himself to the boss, or the phrase that a parent would use in humbly calling the attention of a patron to a promising child. It is always said by a person of inferior social standing to one of superior status. It is *never* used from a person with superior status to a person of lesser social status.

One of the members who was present at that first conference wrote to me recently remembering how Ed had done this. "The members were astounded," she said, "and said to each other, 'How humble our new mission president is.' This is one of my favorite memories of President Okazaki."[7]

Now, Ed knew exactly what he was doing. He wanted to establish a relationship himself as a servant of the people from the very first moment of meeting the members. He would not hide himself or his love for these members behind his title or a nametag or a polished desk in the office. No, from the first moment he was among them, he placed himself at their service, humbly claiming the place of a servant so that he could bring them the gospel. And in doing so, he endeared himself to them.

One of our dear missionaries in Japan was Russell Watanabe, whose father was a rose farmer in Hawaii. Russell has since inherited that farm; and when Hilary Clinton once visited small businesses in Hawaii, she went to his farm. Russell was an excellent missionary, always cheerful and hardworking. He had a thirsty mind and always engaged whomever he was with in conversation to try to better himself, to gain more knowledge, or to understand a Japanese term or a principle of the gospel better. When we left the mission field, all of the missionaries wrote letters of appreciation to Ed as the departing mission president. Elder Watanabe wrote:

> I've had the opportunity to work with flowers since I was a young boy. In a way, I can appreciate the work and care that goes into it. The farmer must make sure to guard the tender shoots against bugs and insects. Fungus and spore diseases are very deadly to the succulent stems, leaves, and petals. Watering and weeding must be taken care of every day as well as frequent pruning to keep the bushes strong and producing. In short, much work and sacrifice is required to obtain the beautiful red rose in the end—work that not only requires daily effort but sometimes holidays and weekends besides. . . .
>
> I see you as the farmers of the Japan-Okinawa Mission.

The mission has really been blessed and we feel we have some real top-notch "experts" leading us. As a missionary, I know of some of the work and sacrifice that is sometimes required on my part to help an investigator, member, or fellow missionary. I appreciate your efforts even more as I see the manner in which you have led us for the past three years.

I have a testimony that we are engaged in a very important work. Einstein said, "Only a life lived for others is a life worthwhile." That is so true. The happiest times on my mission have been experiencing helping others and witnessing others being helped. Little acts of courtesy which you have shown to us . . . are really appreciated and have taught me . . . a great lesson of life—that of sharing. (June 26, 1971.)

More recently, a dear friend, Marion Burns, wrote me that after a talk I had given in San Diego, "a middle-aged man came up to us, opened his wallet, and showed us a photograph of Ed. He had served in your mission and said that Ed was not only a mission president but a second father—then was gone before we caught his name. Imagine how many lives Ed has made better, richer, and holier. Know that we love you, we're proud of you, and proud we had the opportunity to help you and Ed. It seemed a small thing to us at the time, because we just naturally loved you."[8]

Well, this help that he mentions was anything but a small thing. We had been unable to buy a house in Salt Lake City because we were Japanese—this was soon after World War II—and Marion sold us a piece of property that they had been saving for their own house so that we could have a home. We will always love the Burns family and hold their name in honorable remembrance among our children and grandchildren.

But the point I want to make is the importance of finding ways to show love for others through humble service.

I'm not going to urge you to give the missionaries referrals and to friendship new contacts. You all know that. Instead, I want to ask you to see yourselves as bearers of light in a darkened world. Not one of us is perfect. Not one of us is without problems and challenges. But we have the knowledge and the faith and the love to deal with the challenges of sin and sorrow and confusion. Even in affluent and lovely homes there can be challenges of drug and alcohol abuse, of mental illness, and of conflict. People who are poor in worldly goods or who suffer from mental illness or physical disability are also often poor in spirit. We must not judge them because they are poor or deficient in many of the characteristics and blessings that we assume should be readily available to anyone who is disciplined and hardworking. These deficiencies must not be a barrier to our love for these people and especially for their children.

The Savior began his life as a missionary of the gospel by announcing his ministry among those who had great needs. In the synagogue, he read a passage of scripture from Isaiah, which declared: "The Spirit of the Lord is upon me, because he hath anointed me to preach the gospel to the poor; he hath sent me to heal the brokenhearted, to preach deliverance to the captives, and recovering of sight to the blind, to set at liberty them that are bruised." Then to interpret this scripture, he announced that its prophecy was fulfilled by his presence there that day (see Luke 4:18, 21).

The Savior did not serve his mission among people who were already happy, healthy, contented, wealthy, and well-educated. Rather, he looked for those who were in misery and pain, those who lacked hope, were crippled with handicaps, or hungry, despised, and outcast. To serve them, he walked among them, ministering to their needs, not heeding those who criticized him for consorting with those who were known sinners and who broke the laws of ritual purity. Does this tell us something about those swift and secret judgments of the heart that we sometimes make when we encounter people who are different from us in some way? Do we sometimes make judgments, even on a level that we do not consciously recognize, about who is fit to receive the gospel? I think the Savior's message is not only that we must *not* make such judgments but that we must actively position ourselves among those who are the poor, the captives, the blind, and the oppressed if we are to be true ministers of his word.

Just a few blocks south of Temple Square in Salt Lake City lives Narvel Scherzinger, a member of the Church who works at the St. Vincent de Paul soup kitchen, which is sponsored by the Catholic church. "I can sympathize with people who are poor," Narvel said. "I can sympathize with people who are jobless and who want to work." During the Great Depression, his family had no food or money and "had to rely on extended family and friends for help."

Narvel was nominated for a volunteer award by the director of the St. Vincent de Paul soup kitchen because he "exemplifies Christianity." Brother Scherzinger, who serves as part of the Church's program for staffing and supplying the soup kitchen every Saturday, is the "egg man"—he's in charge of cooking the eggs for breakfast. But according to Ann Bero, the director, his real contribution is as a greeter. She says, "He stands at the door and greets people. He's so kind and so sincere. I literally had to cry over the kindness he displayed to the people. He certainly exemplifies [Christ's teaching in the Bible], 'If ye have done it unto the least of these . . . ye have done it unto me.'"

Brother Scherzinger explained that he greets everyone because the people who visit the soup kitchen need more than just food. "They need some kind of recognition that they're somebody," he said.[9]

The greatest recognition that a person is "somebody" is the revealed knowledge that he or she is literally a spiritually begotten child of our Heavenly Father with the potential to ultimately become like God. That Jesus was willing to die for each and every person on the earth is a tremendous understanding that has the power to change the direction of one's life. Many people will not be willing to hear the gospel and so they will not be in a position to accept immediately the great messages that we bear. But in the respect and sincerity of our behavior, we can each be a Brother Scherzinger, who feeds the souls of the poor in Salt Lake City with his kind hello just as he feeds their bodies with the eggs that he cooks each Saturday morning.

Here is one more story that illustrates the urgency of listening to the Spirit as you tune your hearts to transmit Heavenly Father's love to others. Most of you know about origami, the Japanese art of folding a single square sheet of paper into often intricate shapes. A very popular shape is the crane, a Japanese symbol of good luck and happiness.

As a teacher of origami . . . at the LaFarge Lifelong Learning Institute in Milwaukee, Wisconsin, Art Beaudry was asked to represent the school at an exhibit at a large mall in Milwaukee.

He decided to take along a couple hundred folded paper cranes to pass out to people who stopped at his booth.

Before that day, however, something strange happened— a voice told him to find a piece of gold foil paper and make a gold origami crane. The strange voice was so insistent that Art actually found himself rummaging through his collection of origami papers at home until he found one flat, shiny piece of gold foil.

"Why am I doing this?" he asked himself. Art had never worked with the shiny gold paper; it didn't fold as easily or neatly as the crisp multicolored papers. But that little voice kept nudging. Art harrumphed and tried to ignore the voice. "Why gold foil anyway? Paper is much easier to work with," he grumbled.

The voice continued. "Do it! And you must give it away tomorrow to a special person."

By now Art was getting a little cranky. "What special person?" he asked the voice.

"You'll know which one," the voice said.

That evening Art very carefully folded and shaped the unforgiving gold foil until it became as graceful and delicate as a real crane about to take flight. He packed the exquisite bird in the box along with about 200 colorful paper cranes he'd made over the previous few weeks.

The next day at the mall, Art repeatedly demonstrated the art to the many people who stopped at his booth. He was doing so when he looked up and saw a woman standing in front of him. He was unacquainted with her, had never seen her before.

. . . Before he knew what he was doing, his hands were down in the box that contained the supply of paper cranes. There it was, the delicate gold-foil bird he'd labored over the night before. He retrieved it and carefully placed it in the woman's hand.

"I don't know why, but there's a very loud voice inside me telling me I'm supposed to give you this golden crane. The crane is the ancient symbol of peace," Art said simply.

The woman didn't say a word as she slowly cupped her small hand around the fragile bird as if it were alive. When Art looked up at her face, he saw tears filling her eyes, ready to spill out.

Finally, the woman took a deep breath and said, "My husband died three weeks ago. This is the first time I've been out. Today . . ." she wiped her eyes with her free hand, still gently cradling the golden crane with the other.

She spoke very quietly. "Today is our golden wedding anniversary."

Then this stranger said in a clear voice, "Thank you for this beautiful gift. Now I know that my husband is at peace.

Don't you see? That voice you heard, it's the voice of God and this beautiful crane is a gift from Him. It's the most wonderful 50th wedding anniversary present I could have received. Thank you for listening to your heart."[10]

As disciples of Christ, our hearts need to be attuned to accept love and to pass it on. If we are listening, the Spirit will tell us when and how. And as for the question "to whom"? Well, you already know the answer to that question.

## Conclusion

Think for a moment of how we began this chapter with the power of our own names and how it changed our perspective when we did something as simple as to spell them backward. We were reminded of the covenant we entered into when we were baptized and were given the privilege of taking upon us the name of Christ. We have agreed to walk in the way of Jesus, to see with his compassionate eyes, to speak truth and love and comfort as if he were speaking through our mouths, and to be his hands and feet in doing good to each other upon the earth.

Ask yourself this question: If soldiers were searching your house, could they find evidence that you are a Christian? Would a Christian soldier be willing to defend you to the other soldiers because he could tell that you possessed a disciple's love?

Have you ever felt the love of Christ in your heart as John Murdock did? Have you ever felt the love of another human being as Elder Mickelsen felt the love of President Smith and President Benson? Moroni tells us that "charity is the pure love of Christ, and it endureth forever; and whoso is found possessed of it at the last day, it shall be well with him [or her]." Then he counsels us:

> Wherefore, my beloved brethren [and sisters], pray unto the Father with all the energy of heart, that ye may be filled with this love, which he hath bestowed upon all who are true

followers of his Son, Jesus Christ; that ye may become the [children] of God; that when he shall appear we shall be like him. (Moroni 7:48.)

That this precious blessing might be ours is my prayer.

# ENDNOTES

## NOTES TO CHAPTER 1

1. Robert J. Morgan, "What a Friend We Have in Jesus," in *Then Sings My Soul: 150 of the World's Greatest Hymn Stories* (Nashville, TN: Thomas Nelson Publishers, 2003), 130–31.

2. Anonymous, "Leave It to Me," *Sunset with God* (Tulsa, OK: Honor Books, 1996), 14–15.

3. Orson F. Whitney, "Why Don't You Pray?" in *Best-Loved Stories of the LDS People,* edited by Jack M. Lyon, Linda Ririe Gundry, and Jay A. Parry, (Salt Lake City, UT: Deseret Book Company, 1997), 215.

## NOTES TO CHAPTER 2

1. Victor Brown Jr., "Differences," *Ensign,* July 1978, 9.

2. Ibid., 11.

3. "Hearts So Similar," *Ensign,* May 1982, 97; emphasis in original.

4. Robin C. Beadles, "He Made the Blind to See" (Relief Society President, Lomas Ward, Mexico City, Mexico), n.d., photocopy of typescript in my possession, not paginated.

## NOTES TO CHAPTER 3

1. David Heller, *Just Build the Ark and the Animals Will Come* (New York: Villard Books, 1994), 3–4.

2. Women's Conference Memories Scrapbook, Bloomfield Hills Michigan Stake and Westland Stake, 23 May 1996, handmade and compiled by Diane Hubbard and Cathy Montierth.

3. Jackie Ireland, "'Is There Any Reason You Can't Come to Church?'" *Ensign,* July 1992, 22.

4. Odelia M. Fisher, Tallahassee, FL, Letter, 30 December 1997, in my possession.

5. Women's Conference Memories Scrapbook, Bloomfield Hills Michigan Stake and Westland Stake, 23 May 1996, handmade and compiled by Diane Hubbard and Cathy Montierth.

6. Raymond B. Fosdick, "An Invisible Host," in Gordon Owen, *Midnight Meditations* (Salt Lake City, UT: Magazine Printing and Publishing, n.d.), 82.

7. As quoted in *A Thought for Today,* edited by Theron C. Liddle (Salt Lake City: Deseret News Press, 1961), 49.

8. Quoted in *History of the Relief Society* (Salt Lake City: General Board of the Relief Society, 1966), 20.

9. Carol Kuykendall, *Daily Guideposts, 1994* (Carmel, NY: Guideposts, 1993), 145–46.

10. Author Unknown, "The Greatest Moment," in *Love Adds a Little Chocolate,* by Medard Laz, (New York, NY: Warner Books Edition, 1997), 156; emphasis in original.

11. Becki Kearl, "Absolutes," *Exponent II,* 21, no. 1 (n.d., ca. December 1997), 19.

12. Mary Ellen Edmunds, *Thoughts for a Bad Hair Day* (Salt Lake City: Deseret Book Company, 1995), 8.

13. Hannah Cornaby, "What a Dinner We Had That Day," in *Best-Loved Stories of the LDS People,* edited by Jack M. Lyon, Linda Ririe Gundry, and Jay A. Parry, (Salt Lake City, UT: Deseret Book Company, 1997), 138–39.

14. *Teachings of Gordon B. Hinckley* (Salt Lake City: Deseret Book, 1997), 318.

NOTES TO CHAPTER 4

1. Henry Beard and Roy McKie, A *Dictionary of Silly Words about Growing Up* (New York: Workman Publishing, 1988), pages not numbered.

2. As quoted in James Charlton, A *Little Learning Is a Dangerous Thing* (New York: St. Martins Press, 1994), 100.

3. As quoted in James Charlton, A *Little Learning Is a Dangerous Thing,* 15.

4. W. H. Auden and Louis Kronenberger, *The Viking Book of Aphorisms: A Personal Selection* (New York: Dorset Press, 1966 printing), 111.

5. Barbara Knight, "Wise and Otherwise," *Guideposts*, September 1995, 46.

6. Bishop Magee in Marcia & David Kaplan, *Thanks* (1989).

7. Oscar Wilde in Gordon Owen, *This Is Gordon Owen: Scrapbook Collection* (Salt Lake City: Gordon Owen, 1952), 2.

8. Spencer W. Kimball, *The Teachings of Spencer W. Kimball*, compiled by Edward L. Kimball (Salt Lake City: Bookcraft, 1982), 256.

9. No author, *God's Little Devotional Book for Leaders*, compiled by W. B. Freeman Concepts, Inc. (Tulsa, OK: Honor Books, Inc., 1997), 175.

10. Anne Osborn Poelman, *The Amulek Alternative* (Salt Lake City, UT: Deseret Book Company, 1997), 9–11.

11. Marion D. Hanks, "Was He Relevant?" *Speeches of the Year Pamphlet* (Provo, UT: BYU Press, December 17, 1968), 7–8.

## NOTES TO CHAPTER 5

1. Demi, *The Empty Pot* (New York: Henry Holt and Company, 1900), n.p.

## NOTES TO CHAPTER 6

1. H. Jackson Brown Jr., comp., *Live and Learn and Pass It On, Vol. II* (Nashville, TN: Rutledge Hill Press, 1955), 73.

2. Malcolm Forbes, in *To Your Success: Thoughts to Give Wings to Your Work and Your Dreams*, compiled by Dan Zadra (Woodinville, Washington: Compendium, Inc., 1994), 83.

3. In *The New Book of Christian Quotations*, compiled by Tony Castle (New York: Crossroads, York, 1983), 9.

4. John Wooden, in *To Your Success: Thoughts to Give Wings to Your Work and Your Dreams*, compiled by Dan Zadra (Woodinville, Washington: Compendium, Inc., 1983), 24.

5. George F. Richards, *Improvement Era*, November 1946.

6. Hunter, "The God That Doest Wonders," *Ensign*, May 1989, 16.

7. Connie Kent, "Be Pleasant," *Church News*, August 7, 1993, 15.

8. Myrtle "Cookie" Potter, "His Mysterious Ways," *Guideposts*, May 1998, 9.

9. President Hunter, "Follow the Son of God," *Ensign*, November 1994, 88.

10. Toko Fujii, "Sacramento Honors Sughiara Who Saved Jews during World War II," *Pacific Citizen*, 17 February–2 March 1995, 4. In my possession.

11. Frances R. Havergal, 1874, "Take My Life," *The Lutheran Hymnal,* No. 400. (St. Louis, MO: Concordia Publishing House, 1941).

12. Suzanne C. Stewart, "Sink or Swim," *Ensign,* January 1994, 44.

## Notes to Chapter 7

1. Jeni Broberg Holzapfel and Richard Neitzel Holzapfel, *Sisters at the Well: Women and the Life and Teachings of Jesus* (Salt Lake City: Bookcraft, 1993), 117.

2. Ibid., 118.

3. Launie Severinsen, "Thoughts of Martha and Mary," 22 May 1984.

4. Unknown, in W. B. Freeman Concepts, Inc., comp., *God's Little Devotional Book on Success* (Tulsa, OK: Honor Books, Inc., 1997), 183.

5. Launie Severinsen, "The Gift of Charity," 31 May 1983; revised 13 May 1992, 3.

6. Ibid., 135.

7. Ibid., 136.

8. Ibid., 136.

9. Ibid., 139.

10. Ibid., 134–35.

## Notes to Chapter 8

1. George Q. Cannon, sermon on 1 March 1891; in Brian H. Stuy, *Collected Discourses,* 2:185.

2. Delbert L. Stapley, conference address, 5 April 1975, as quoted in *Church News,* 8 August 1992, 2.

3. Jerrie Hurd, *Leaven: 150 Women in Scripture Whose Lives Lift Ours* (Murray, UT: Aspen Books, 1995), 118–20.

4. Perry H. Cunningham, "Activity in the Church," *Encyclopedia of Mormonism,* 4 vols. (New York: Macmillan Publishing Company, 1992), vol. 1, 15.

5. Melissa Aniello, "Celebrating Differences," 2 May 1993, Tualitan Oregon Stake, 2–4. Photocopy of typescript in my possession. Used by permission.

6. Mildred N. Hoyer, as quoted in *Guideposts,* June 1995, 13.

7. Linda J. Roberts, "Let Me Have Your Shoes," *The Ensign,* October 1993, 45.

8. Jerry W. Richardson, as quoted in *Guideposts,* April 1996, 36.

9. Larry Dossey, "When Science Investigates Prayer," *Guideposts*, June 1995, 37–39.

## NOTES TO CHAPTER 9

1. Joanie E. Yoder, "Knowing God Personally," *Our Daily Bread*, March, April, May 1995, Friday, March 17.

2. Jeffrey R. Holland, *Christ and the New Covenant* (Salt Lake City: Deseret Book Company, 1997) 23–24 (italics in original).

3. Women's Conference Memories Scrapbook, Bloomfield Hills Michigan Stake and Westland Stake, 23 May 1996, handmade and compiled by Diane Hubbard and Cathy Montierth.

4. *Teachings of Gordon B. Hinckley* (Salt Lake City: Deseret Book Company, 1997), 574.

5. Joseph Smith, *Teachings of the Prophet Joseph Smith*, sel. Joseph Fielding Smith, (Salt Lake City: Deseret Book, Co., 1938), 174.

6. Leon Joseph Sueness in *The New Book of Christian Quotations*, compiled by Tony Castle (New York: Crossroads, New York, 1983), 36.

7. No author, *Coffee Break with God* (Tulsa, OK: Honor Books, Inc., 1996), 114–15.

8. William Arthur Ward, as quoted in James Charlton, *A Little Learning Is a Dangerous Thing* (New York: St. Martins Press, 1994), 61.

## NOTES TO CHAPTER 10

1. Haddon W. Robinson, "Doing the Impossible," *Our Daily Bread*, January 1999, January 11.

2. President Gordon B. Hinckley, priesthood leadership meeting, Vacaville/Santa Rosa Regional Conference, May 20, 1995, *Church News*.

3. Wallace E. Gibson, "A Protective Net," *Church News*, 19 June 1993, 16.

4. George Q. Cannon, *My First Mission* (Faith Promoting Series) (Salt Lake City: Juvenile Instructor Office, 1979), 18.

5. John Murdock, "Journal," *Utah Genealogical and Historical Magazine* 28 (April 1937): 61, as quoted in Blaine M. Yorgason, "the Prophet Joseph's Grand Design," *Latter-day Digest*, vol. 2, no. 4 (August 1993), 68.

6. Janet Peterson, "Friend to Friend," *Friend*, August 1993, 6.

7. Sumie Linnett, letter to Chieko N. Okazaki, 18 July 1995.

8. Marion Burns, letter, 17 May 1995.

9. Amy Donaldson, "'Egg Man' Honored for Service," *Deseret News,* 24 May 1993, B-1, B-2.

10. Patricia Lorenz, "The Golden Crane," in *A 3rd Serving of Chicken Soup for the Soul,* by Jack Canfield, Mark Victor Hansen (Deerfield Beach, FL: Health Communications, Inc., 1996), 140–142.

# INDEX